FLORENCE KELLEY

Florence Kelley

FLORENCE KELLEY

The Making of a Social Pioneer

By

Dorothy Rose Blumberg

AUGUSTUS M. KELLEY · *Publishers*
NEW YORK · 1966

To
My mother and my husband
with love and thanks.

TABLE OF CONTENTS

ACKNOWLEDGEMENTS

Among the pleasures of research are the enthusiasm and courtesy with which the researcher is greeted. This was invariably my experience, both personally and through correspondence, during the several years of gathering material.

My thanks go first to the librarians at Columbia University, especially to Rita Keckeissen and John Waddell, who were never too busy to help me ferret out an obscure reference; to Josephine M. Tharpe, Reference Librarian, and the archivists of Cornell University, who placed files and records at my disposal; to Josephine L. Harper, Manuscripts Librarian at the Wisconsin State Historical Society, for locating and making available the Ely and Lloyd letters; to Jean McNiece in the Manuscript Division of the New York Public Library; to Dr. David C. Mearns, Chief of the Manuscript Division of the Library of Congress, and to his staff; and to Professor G. Obichkin, Director of the Institute of Marxism-Leninism in Moscow, for the microfilm copies of Florence Kelley's letters to Engels.

I am also grateful to Louise Heinze of the Tamiment Library for assistance with the early records of the Socialist Labor Party; to the librarians of the Historical Society of Pennsylvania and the Philadelphia Public Library; to the custodians of the Race Street Friends Meeting House in Philadelphia; to the archivists of the Swarthmore College Peace Collection; and to the registrars of the Universities of Zürich and Heidelberg.

I also want to thank Professor Henry F. Graff, head of the History Department of Columbia University, who read part of the manuscript and made a number of valuable suggestions.

And finally, my deepest gratitude goes to my husband, who despite a heavy schedule of his own, found time to read, criticize and tirelessly encourage these pages to a successful conclusion.

D. R. B.

New York, 1964

LIST OF ILLUSTRATIONS

FOREWORD

In the long history of the struggle against child labor in America, the person who made the most consistent and effective contribution was Florence Kelley. Starting with the premise that children belong in schools, not in factories, mills and mines, she gave most of her life to an unremitting struggle for legislation prohibiting the employment of children under sixteen, and for compulsory education until that age was reached.

During the first thirty years of the present century, her activities took her into virtually every state in the Union. As General Secretary of the National Consumers' League she appeared at dozens of legislative and Congressional hearings; buttonholed Senators, Congressmen and Cabinet members; addressed women's clubs, parent-teacher associations, church groups, social work conferences, trade union gatherings; and in between found time for innumerable reports, magazine and journal articles, and letters to friends and to the press.

Nor were her interests confined to the need for protective legislation. She was one of the founders of the National Association for the Advancement of Colored People; a vice-president of the National Woman Suffrage Association; held various offices in the Intercollegiate Socialist Society; was a member of the Board of Control of Labor Standards in army clothing during World War I; and attended the Women's Peace Conference in Zürich after the war. Wherever she went her opinions were respected and her advice and suggestions sought.

She did not live to see her dearest wish fulfilled—ratification of the Child Labor Amendment, which Congress had passed in 1924. At the time of her death in 1932 only six states had ratified, although during the next several years a number of additional states took action, persuaded by the Depression and encouraged by the New Deal. But while the requisite thirty-six were never obtained, a partial victory was scored with the passage of the Fair Labor Standards Act in 1938. The Act included a sixteen-year minimum age for child labor "in interstate commerce," and thus a national minimum protection for children was at last secured.

Despite her many years of selfless service, her wide involvements and her memorable influence on so many of her contemporaries, the name of Florence Kelley today evokes only the vaguest recognition or none at all. Surely we cannot afford to let such a vivid, dynamic person disappear from historical view. "It will be a sad loss to the world," wrote Lillian Wald shortly after Mrs. Kelley's death, "if the story of that ardent crusader is not retold to coming generations, for her times knew none more effective. She made her generation think!"

This book is an attempt to retell part of that story—to examine in particular the background and the early influences and experiences that made Florence Kelley the woman she became. Much of the telling, fortunately, can be in her own words, which so well convey the delightful blend of wit, scorn, tact and temper that were hers. Her writings, her speeches, and especially her letters, reveal her unusual range of interest, her boundless compassion, and above all the social philosophy that supported her "enlistment for the duration" in the struggle for a just social order.

In an age when the Darwinian notion of "survival of the fittest" was so widely misapplied to provide a convenient salve for conscience, Florence Kelley boldly challenged the comforting assumption, and laid bare the ugly industrial machinery that was grinding out poverty and all its attendant social ills. No cause was too unpopular if she believed in it, no situation too distasteful if she felt it could be aided by her presence. She spent herself recklessly, and so she always had an infinite amount to give.

Perhaps it is time to make the acquaintance once more of this remarkable person, who was such an inspiration to her generation, and might be so again to ours.

CHAPTER I

Roots and Branches

*Free Soilers and Revolutionary ancestors, Quakers
and Abolitionists and Non-Conformists, family figures
who had put their consciences to the tests of both
endurance and action. Such (was) . . . the heritage of
one Philadelphia child of sixty years ago.*

Florence Kelley[1]

Conscience, endurance, action—there could perhaps be no
better summing up of what went into the making of Florence
Kelley. It was an impressive heritage, and one that demanded
as much from as it conferred upon the little "Philadelphia
child."

The family line can be traced back as far as a seventeenth
century Thomas Kelley of Londonderry, in northern Ireland.
Why this "first of three generations of Thomases" decided to
emigrate is not known. Ireland had suffered heavily under
Cromwell's "pacification," and the accession of Charles II had
not appreciably lightened the burden. Many who could had left
the country. Kelley stayed on until 1662, then sailed for
America. Settling on the New Jersey bank of the Delaware
River at a place then called Ruff's landing, he acquired land
and apparently prospered.

---

[1] "My Philadelphia," *The Survey*, Oct. 1, 1926, p. 11. This is the first of four
autobiographical sketches by Mrs. Kelley which appeared in *The Survey* under the
general heading "Notes of Sixty Years." The others are: "When Co-education was
Young," Feb. 1, 1927; "My Novitiate," April 1, 1927; "I Go to Work," June 1,
1927. Free use has been made of this material throughout.

Josephine Goldmark's appreciative biography, *Impatient Crusader,* The Life Story
of Florence Kelley, (Urbana, 1953) deals primarily with Mrs. Kelley's career as
General Secretary of the National Consumers League (1899-1932). It does, however,
contain some useful information for the earlier period.

By the time of the Revolutionary War, in which Major John Kelley, son of Thomas the third, served at the head of a company he himself had raised,[2] the family had moved to Salem, New Jersey. Also living in West Jersey was a small group of French Huguenots who had fled persecution many years before. Among them were the Casteaus, whose daughter Elizabeth became John's wife. A son, David Kelley, born in 1784, grew up to marry Hannah Darrah. The Darrahs had been early comers to Bucks County, and Hannah's father, William, had been an officer in the French and Indian Wars and in the Revolutionary War. To Hannah and David were born four children, of whom the youngest, William Darrah Kelley, was Florence Kelley's father.

William Kelley's wife, Caroline Bartram Bonsall, brought strong Quaker influences into the family, and an eminent ancestor. The first Bonsalls recorded in America, Richard and his wife Mary, came from the Quaker community in Derbyshire, England, to the one in Darby, Pennsylvania, in 1683. Richard's son Benjamin married Mary Bartram, daughter of John Bartram, the renowned colonial botanist, close friend of Benjamin Franklin, and one of the founders of the American Philosophical Society. Their son James became the father of Henry Lummis Bonsall, whose fourth child, Caroline, was Florence Kelley's mother.[3]

Although Henry Bonsall had married "out of meeting," the family remained within the Quaker community and tradition. When his wife Hannah died in 1833, and he followed her five years later, Caroline was adopted (although keeping her surname) by the Quaker Isaac Pugh and his wife Elizabeth Kay Pugh of Germantown. With no children of their own, the Pughs over the years had taken four little girls into their home. "Never were mother and father more tenderly loved by children of flesh and blood than these," and they were as fondly remembered as grandparents by young Florence, who spent some of the happiest days of her childhood in their home.

---

[2] Nicholas Kelley to James Weber Linn, March 26, 1935. In the Swarthmore Peace Collection, Swarthmore, Pa.

[3] Genealogy Record, Bonsall Family Papers. Columbia University Manuscript Library.

William Darrah Kelley

Caroline Bonsall Kelley

Susan B. Anthony

"Grandaunt" Sarah Pugh
(Swarthmore Peace Collection)

Lucretia Mott

Elizabeth Pugh's family were Unitarians who had come to Pennsylvania from England in 1794. A fellow voyager was their good friend Joseph Priestley, the famous chemist, unorthodox minister and libertarian, who in 1791 had lost his chapel, his laboratory and almost his life because of his outspoken and continued support first of the American Revolution, then of the French Revolution.[4]

History, then, in the Pugh and Kelley homes was not something past and done with—read in a book, framed and hung on a wall, or laid away in boxes. It was lived with and a part of living, alive as each new day. The conversation around the table as often recounted a family event of fifty or a hundred years before as of yesterday; and to attentive little Florence, John Bartram or Joseph Priestley might well have just stepped from the room.

Within this close-knit family, the two who wrote themselves large on her youthful consciousness were her father and Sarah Pugh, sister of her "adopted" grandfather.

Grandaunt Sarah was remembered as slight of figure and sparing of speech, her silver hair cut short under her close-fitting Quaker cap in "silent protest against the compulsory use of long hair for women." Born in 1800, she had as a young woman taught for some years at the Friends' School at Twelfth Street Meeting House, later opening her own girls' school on Walnut Street.[5]

Though opposed to slavery by Quaker precept and practice, she took no part in the growing abolitionist protest until in 1835 she heard the Englishman George Thompson deliver a stirring plea for immediate emancipation. Still retaining her teaching post, she joined the Female Anti-Slavery Society founded by Lucretia Mott, and remained active in the organization until it disbanded in 1870. When in the spring of 1838

---

[4] The mob chose Bastille Day, July 14, 1791, for its assault on Priestley's house and laboratory. *Memoirs of Dr. Joseph Priestley, to the year 1795 written by himself; with a continuation to the time of his decease, by his son Joseph Priestley* (1806). The reference to the Kays sailing with him is from *The Survey*, Oct. 1, 1926, p. 53. Priestley does not mention it.

[5] *Memorial of Sarah Pugh: A Tribute of Respect from her Cousins* (Philadelphia, 1888). Unless otherwise noted, biographical material on Sarah Pugh is taken from the *Memorial*.

the Pennsylvania Hall meeting place of the Anti-Slavery Convention of American Women was burned out by a mob, she invited the delegates to reconvene in her school room. The following year she helped circulate abolition petitions to be presented to Congress and the State Legislature. In 1840 she represented the Pennsylvania Female Anti-Slavery Society at the World Anti-Slavery Convention in London, where the women delegates (joined by an indignant William Lloyd Garrison) were made to sit in the gallery "behind a bar and a curtain"; and her name as secretary of the Pennsylvania delegation appears on the resolution that protested this treatment.[6]

At the age of fifty she gave up teaching to devote her full time "to promoting the anti-slavery movement, peace, woman suffrage, the single standard of morals for men and women, and free trade."[7] A year later, what began as a European pleasure trip with Isaac and Elizabeth Pugh, turned into a speaking tour in behalf of abolition that kept her in the British Isles for almost two years.

After the outbreak of the Civil War her energies were directed toward care for Negroes who, freed from slavery in the wake of the Union advance, had been left destitute. She helped organize collections of clothing and food sent by the Pennsylvania Freedman's Association to the Sea Islands off the coast of South Carolina. In April, 1866, she herself made a trip to the Islands, where at St. Helena, by the heroic efforts of Dr. Laura Towne and Ellen Murray, a viable, educated community of freedmen had been patiently brought into being.

She was equally dedicated to the struggle for women's rights, and was a lifelong friend of both Lucretia Mott and Susan B. Anthony. Her participation in this movement during the decade before the Civil War is reflected in her diary entries—a lecture in 1851 by Mrs. Mott on Women's Rights; an "accidental dinner party," also at Mrs. Mott's, in 1854 at which Ernestine Rose spoke on "woman's rights and other ultraisms"; a Women's Rights Convention in Boston in 1855 which heard an address by Theodore Parker, and another in New

---

[6] The text of the petition is found in the *Memorial*, p. 24. The reference to "bar and curtain" is from Yuri Suhl, *Ernestine Rose and the Battle for Human Rights* (New York, 1959), p. 99.

[7] *The Survey, op. cit.*, p. 54.

York in 1860 with Elizabeth Cady Stanton the principal speaker.

After the war the women's rights struggle absorbed even more of her time. The split in the suffrage movement that had taken place in 1869 caused her particular anxiety.[8] In May, 1871, she wrote of attending meetings in New York of each of the two branches, in the "hope that by going some differences I wished to understand might be solved." They weren't, but the fact did not dim her admiration and love for Miss Anthony, or halt the regular contributions to the cause from her small savings.

At the same time her concern grew for the social and legal inequities suffered generally by women, a concern that she shared with many of her English friends. While one of them, Mrs. Josephine Butler, was writing to Queen Victoria and Parliament "against the segregation of women in lock hospitals" under the Contagious Diseases Act,[9] Sarah Pugh in her seventy-fourth year was once again circulating petitions, this time successfully, against a proposition in the State Legislature to license prostitution.

Although her trips from home were now less frequent, she continued to maintain a large correspondence. Over the years her letters had gone out regularly to John Stuart Mill, Richard Cobden and John Bright, Lady Stanley of Alderley, the Duchess of Sutherland (whom she had visited in London) and many others; and she still spent many hours each day tracing her thoughts in a firm, delicate script.

If any of these letters still exist, they have yet to be gathered together in printed form. But the diary excerpts that remain speak eloquently for her. They reveal a woman of simplicity, modesty and humor, in no way bound by trivial convention

[8] The split came over whether the Equal Rights Association should continue to work for women's rights in general or for suffrage alone. In support of the wider program Miss Anthony and Mrs. Stanton organized the National Woman Suffrage Association. Some months later Lucy Stone and Julia Ward Howe, among others, set up the American Woman Suffrage Association which confined itself to the issue of suffrage. Eleanor Flexner, *A Century of Struggle* (Cambridge, 1959), pp. 152-53. The rift was healed in 1890.

[9] Under the guise of protecting garrisons and naval stations, the Act permitted the arrest and compulsory examination of women suspected of venereal disease, and their detention in hospitals if found affected. Anne Henrietta Martin, "Josephine Elizabeth Butler," *Encyclopedia Britannica*, 1960 ed., IV, 463.

or ritual; one whose Quaker devotion to principle and to humanity animated all her being; who consciously strove to free herself from petty or narrow considerations, to "judge men by their actions, not their opinions," and to see political or social problems in more than their immediate aspect. That by quiet discussion as well as consistent example she should pass these ideals on to her adoring grandniece was the most natural thing in the world.

When William Darrah Kelley was born, on April 12, 1814, his family was still living at 227 North Second Street, in the Philadelphia district then known as Northern Liberties. The early years were not easy. His father, long a leading watchmaker and jeweler, had suffered severe losses during the crisis that followed the War of 1812. These David Kelley might have weathered had he not also endorsed a note for his brother-in-law, who failed to meet the obligation. The strain, both physical and financial, was too much. Kelley Senior saw his business swept away, and shortly thereafter collapsed and died in the street of apoplexy at the age of thirty-two.[10]

After the creditors were satisfied there was almost nothing left. With three little girls and two-year old William to support, Hannah Kelley opened a boarding house not far from her old home, and with the help of her husband's brother managed to keep the family together. But times remained hard, and at the age of eleven William left school to go to work. For the next several years he was variously employed—at a dollar a week in a lottery office (respectable enough in those days), as errand boy in a bookstore, by an umbrella maker, and as copy reader in the printing office of Jesper Harding. In this last his hours were cruelly long, in winter from six in the morning till eight at night, in summer from light until dark; and the green tea the little fellow chewed—on the advice of a fellow worker—to keep himself awake, only added to the strain and fatigue that left him with a lifelong "nervous excitability."

[10] The biographical sketch of William Darrah Kelley is drawn from *Speeches, Addresses and Letters of William D. Kelley* (Philadelphia, 1872), *passim;* Mrs. Kelley's *Survey* sketches; Hugh T. Leffler, "William Darrah Kelley," *Dictionary of American Biography,* (New York, 1943), pp. 299-300; and L. B. Brockett, *Men of Our Day* (Philadelphia, 1872), pp. 495-503.

At thirteen, taking with him his father's tools which had escaped the sheriff's sale, young William was apprenticed to the jewelry manufacturing firm of Richards and Dubosq for the customary seven years. Here, while his natural skill grew and developed, he found time to help establish a Youth's Library which later became the Pennsylvania Library Institute, and to join "with the journeymen of [his] and other trades in promoting the recognition of the ten-hour system."[11]

His apprenticeship completed in the depression year of 1834, he might still have found a job had he not already drawn unfavorable notice by organizing Democratic workmen in support of President Jackson's fight against the Bank of the United States. To Philadelphia's Whigs and conservative Democrats this was outrageous behavior. The doors of employment were so securely closed to young Kelley that he had to leave home. Making his way to Boston, he found a job with the jewelry firm of Clark and Curry.

For the next four years he worked diligently, displaying unusual ingenuity and artistry; a set of gold cups made for the Imam of Muscat won his employers a gold medal from the Massachusetts Mechanics' Association. In his spare time he pursued his self-education, reading Emerson's essays and the sermons of William Ellery Channing, writing a little, and acquiring a reputation as a speaker. At a meeting in Faneuil Hall he made so favorable an impression that George Bancroft, then Collector of the Port, invited him to use his library. Determined to remain independent, the young man tactfully refused all proffers of assistance, including Bancroft's advice to apply for a Harvard scholarship.

Returning to his native city in 1839, he began to read law in the office of Colonel James Page, a local leader of the Democratic Party, and two years later was admitted to the Philadelphia bar. In 1845 he was appointed prosecutor of pleas for Philadelphia, in 1847 judge of the court of common pleas.

Meanwhile he had married Isabella Tennant of Baltimore, who bore him a daughter, Harriette. Very little else is known

---

[11] William D. Kelley, *Speeches*, etc., *op. cit.*, p. 279.

of this union, which proved to be a short duration. In 1854 Judge Kelley married Caroline Bonsall.

The following year the judicial office he held was made elective, and he was chosen to serve for the next ten years. He did not complete his term of office. In 1854 a Democratic Congress under Franklin Pierce surrendered to Southern pressure and passed the Kansas-Nebraska bill repealing the Missouri Compromise. To the many Democrats who opposed extension of slavery this was nothing short of betrayal, and they expressed their disgust by walking out of the party. With them went Judge Kelley, who resigned his post forthwith. Two years later an unsolicited nomination as Congressional candidate for the Fourth District placed him on Frémont's Republican Party ticket. Losing in the general party defeat, he returned to the practice of law.

In 1860 he took a prominent part in the Republican National Convention in Chicago. He was a member of the Committee which notified Lincoln of his nomination, and in the Lincoln victory on November 6 was elected to Congress by a narrow margin. Thus began a distinguished career in the House of Representatives that lasted thirty years and earned him the title "Father of the House."

His relationship with President Lincoln was not only that of a dependable party supporter but of a trusted friend. He visited the White House often enough to describe himself as "an habitué of the Executive Chamber"—once especially to urge the replacement of General McClellan in the fall of 1862—and was among those "with whom the President had confidences and secrets." Lincoln was impressed with the Congressman's talents as a vote-getter even in an off-year election. Judge Kelley in turn considered Lincoln "the wisest radical of us all."[12]

Member of the House Ways and Means Committee for twenty years and chairman for two (1883-1885), his "dominant, absorbing passion" was the development of America's

[12] William D. Kelley in *Reminiscences of Abraham Lincoln by Distinguished Men of His Time,* ed. Allen Thorndike Rice (New York, 1888), pp. 255-91; Carl Sandburg, *Abraham Lincoln, The War Years* (New York, 1939), III, group portrait including Kelley, opposite p. 403; John G. Nicolay and John Hay, *Abraham Lincoln, A History* (Century, 1890), IX, 62. Material in this paragraph is also in Sandburg, *op. cit.,* I and III, *passim.*

natural resources, the development and diversification of her industries. He had originally been an advocate of free trade and of a tariff for revenue only; but the depression of 1857, together with a study of English labor conditions—the low estate of which he attributed to the British free trade policy—combined to turn him into a staunch and vocal protectionist. Perhaps equally influential were the economic theories of his "venerable friend and teacher" Henry C. Carey, with whom he maintained close personal ties of respect and affection. Even so, as he wrote in 1871, "It was not easy to abandon opinions I had cherished through so many years . . . and . . . accept the opposite system, that of protection, which I had so often denounced as false, selfish and exclusive."[13]

He was deeply troubled that the Civil War had left the South an economic shambles. The damage must be repaired, he felt, by rapid and thorough industrialization rather than by seeking to rebuild the worn-out plantation system. He carried this message personally to the Southern states, speaking in a number of cities of the glowing opportunities opening up now that the "hell-born institution of slavery" had been defeated. He was not always well received. In Mobile, the *Times* had been whipping up a lynch spirit for several days before his scheduled address. On signal, a riot broke out while he was speaking; one man was killed and another wounded, although the Congressman himself escaped injury.[14]

Legal emancipation for women was as dear to his heart as bodily emancipation of the slave. An early and long-time friend of Susan B. Anthony, he spoke often on platforms with her, and chaired such Women's Rights conventions as were held in Washington. When the House sponsor of a suffrage amendment moved up to the Senate, Congressman Kelley assumed the sponsorship.[15]

---

[13] W. D. Kelley, *Speeches,* etc., *op. cit.,* p. xii. His insistent demand, on the floor of Congress and in many of his other speeches and writings, in favor of tariff protection of the iron and steel industry, earned him the nickname "Pig-Iron Kelley." He often received letters addressed to the "Hon. P. I. Kelley." "William D. Kelley," *Harper's Weekly,* Jan. 16, 1890, p. 52.

[14] Kelley, *Speeches,* etc., pp. 172-73.

[15] Ida Husted Harper, *The Life and Work of Susan B. Anthony* (Indianapolis, 1894), I, 233.

Widely traveled in Europe as well as in America, he made of his trips useful explorations into the economics and politics of the places visited, and the opinions of personages encountered; and frequently published his findings. One such expedition was a three-months tour of England and the Continent in the summer of 1879, during which he asked for and received an interview with Bismarck. The Chancellor spoke fully and freely about Germany's new fiscal policies, and found agreement with the Congressman on the subject of protective tariffs. This conversation Judge Kelley considered so significant that he reported it in detail in one of a series of letters to the Philadelphia *Times,* an act which aroused something of a storm in Germany and caused no little discomfort to the American ambassador, Andrew D. White, who had arranged the interview.[16]

In the letters he permitted himself one personal note: "Coming abroad as I did, in the pursuit of health . . ." This was an allusion to the malignancy, rarely mentioned, from which he had been suffering for some years. In the spring of 1883 he underwent a painful operation for removal of a cancerous growth in his cheek, but the relief afforded was only temporary. Although he returned to Congress in the fall, and was to serve through three more terms, the deadly malady finally had its way, and he died in Washington on January 9, 1890.

The courage with which he continued to carry out his elective duties in spite of pain and failing physical powers was as characteristic as the blunt self-assurance that so often infuriated his political opponents. Both sprang from his profound sense of obligation to the welfare—as he saw it—of his constituents and his country, and it was on this basis that he addressed himself to issues. Once the issues had been determined and a stand taken, the course he then followed was to him

---

[16] William D. Kelley, *Letters from Europe: Six Letters Written to the Philadelphia Times During the Summer of 1879, With Notes by the author* (Philadelphia, 1879). Ambassador White, on leave as president of Cornell University, had cautioned Representative Kelley to be discreet in whatever he reported of this interview. Kelley's full account, including Bismarck's frank references to his colleagues, stirred up much indignation in the German press. Kelley excused himself by saying it was "necessary for the world to know what the great chancellor had said on so important a subject." *Autobiography of Andrew D. White* (New York, 1922), I, 581-85.

only the logical outgrowth of established conviction. It was this rigorous adherence to the principled cause that was his chief legacy to his daughter Florence.

CHAPTER II

The Twig is Bent

Shortly after his second marriage Judge Kelley built a large, comfortable house in West Philadelphia, "four miles as the crow flies from Independence Hall." The site, now occupied by the clinic buildings of the Hospital for Women and Children at Parrish and Forty-first Streets, was in those days so isolated that it could be reached only "by stage and horse car."

Misfortune marked the early years of the marriage. Of the eight fine, healthy children that Caroline Kelley bore, only three grew to adulthood. Five of the six little girls died in a period of twelve years, "sacrificed . . . to the prevailing ignorance of the hygiene of infancy, . . . from infections now recognized as preventable." Surviving were the oldest child William D., Jr., the youngest, Albert Bartram, and the third child and second daughter, Florence Molthrop, born September 12, 1859.

Although too young to have shared "the terror of impending loss," the little girl could not but sense her mother's "settled, gentle melancholy" which even the strong Quaker faith was unable to dispel. Caroline Kelley moves briefly through her daughter's memoirs, a shadowy figure, stricken by her losses yet continuing to maintain a household and an open door of hospitality for the sake of the remaining children.

With her mother struggling against sickness and death, and her father away during the long Congressional sessions, little Florence was left largely to her own devices. It was a lonely childhood, though not, as she recalls it, an unhappy one. The wide, tree-shaded lawn gave ample space for play, and there were frequent visits to the Germantown home of her grandparents the Pughs.

Her earliest recorded recollection—she was just five and a half—is of being at her grandparents' and witnessing their grief and shock at news of President Lincoln's assassination:

> It was a sunny day, and a robin ran over the close cropped, bright green grass of the back garden. Nothing could have been gayer. How different the breakfast table! My taciturn grandfather's formidable features . . . looked that day as if chiseled in stone. My grandmother, serene in all my previous experience with her, looked shattered and was silent throughout the meal. After breakfast she said to me: "In time of grief it is well for families to be together. You and I will drive to your home." Then in a voice of utter sadness she added, "My child, President Lincoln is dead. He was shot last night."
>
> We drove in silence the seven miles to our parents' home in West Philadelphia. The sidewalks were empty. People were draping their doors in mourning and shutters were closed as if Death had entered every home.[1]

The Civil War left other remembered traces on the family. Florence's two uncles, Henry and William Bonsall, had seen active service, the latter as a surgeon. Both contracted tuberculosis from their experiences and died of it some years later, one of them at the Kelley home.

Judge Kelley himself, just completing his first term in the House of Representatives, had answered Lincoln's emergency call of September, 1862. In spite of Congressional immunity he had joined an artillery company shortly before the battle of Antietam, where he had been in charge of the spare guns and sick horses of one of the batteries, and had carried messages for the officers. While he took no part in any engagement, "his huge musket and light blue army overcoat and cap greatly impressed us even when they hung in a closet long after the war."[2]

The issues of the war, too, remained live topics of discussion within the family circle. Grandaunt Sarah never could reconcile herself to the fact that her brother Isaac had not volunteered their home as a way-station on the Underground Railroad, and frequently said so. Nor did she, as her niece observed,

---

[1] "My Philadelphia," *The Survey*, Oct. 1, 1926, p. 7.
[2] *Dictionary of American Biography, op. cit.;* Kelley, *Reminiscences of Abraham Lincoln,* etc., p. 273; *The Survey, op. cit.,* p. 8.

FLORENCE KELLEY AS A LITTLE GIRL

Aged 3

Aged 4½

Aged 6

Aged 14

The Kelley home at 41st and Parrish (formerly Myrtle) Streets

ever depart from her custom of not using sugar or cotton because these were produced by slaves.

Not meaning to be impertinent, I once said, "Aunt Sarah, does Thee really think any slaves were freed because Thee did not use sugar or cotton?" Perfectly tranquil was her reply: "Dear child, I can never know that any slave was personally helped; but I had to live with my own conscience."[3]

Lessons in reading, begun by her father when the little girl was seven, combined social problems with ABC's. For text Judge Kelley used a graphically illustrated book showing the miserable existence of youngsters, no older than his daughter, at work in the brickyards of England. He also told of slave children sold away from their parents, and of "bound" boys and girls working out long years of indenture. Her mother and grandmother protested against "darkening the mind of a young child with such dismal ideas," but with the example of her father's own harsh boyhood before her the stories became rather an illumination.

By the following year she was considered ready for school, but attendance was to prove at best a hazardous and uncertain pleasure. Her first experience in the fall of 1867 at "a delightful little school in Germantown" lasted only a short time and "ended in bed and a winter of rheumatism." The next year, however, she was able to attend the Friends' Central School at 1520 Race Street, in Philadelphia, long enough at least to "garner several precious memories."

One of these was of the Fourth Day morning service, when through the Race Street entrance the children filed into the Meeting House for an hour of worship. The younger girls and boys sat in the eastern and western sectors of the gallery on uncushioned benches, the older classes in the east and west banks of seats on the main floor. The central ground floor section was reserved for the adults, who in those years, and indeed until well into the present century, came dressed in plain Quaker garb, the women in stiff bonnets over their white net caps, the men in the traditional broad-brimmed hats.

To nine-year old Florence on the hard wooden seat "the

---

[3] *Ibid.*, p. 4.

weekly hour seemed endless, brightened only by the flickering hope that the Spirit might begin promptly."[4] There was no clock on the meeting-house wall, timepieces being considered unseemly distractions; yet the meeting generally "broke" at the appointed half-past eleven. This was due not so much to an obliging Spirit as to Friend Robert Biddle who sat in meditation in the first row, head bowed over his walking stick in the knob of which was a well-regulated watch.[5]

From the same year she records another memory, this a painful one. The horse-car that took her to and from school ran past "a large, forbidding looking building," the Manayunk textile mill. There, each midday, might be seen "little skinny girls waiting on the sidewalk before closed doors, . . . the 'hands' returning from their noon half-hour for dinner."

The Friends' School experience came to an abrupt end when an attack of scarlet fever, "due doubtless to travel in the filthy horse-cars," sent her back to the sick-room. Recovery left her without after effects, but there was to be no more public school for some four years.

Such recurring obstacles to learning became in the end a spur to the little girl. She was barely ten when she became aware of her father's library as more than just another room. Methodically she set herself to read, "starting at the ceiling at the southwest corner of the study," and finishing the bottom shelves some six or seven years later.

For the "lonely child deeply ashamed of having no school experience" it was indeed a "huge, indigestible, intellectual meal"; but she went at it doggedly, although many of the volumes were beyond her comprehension. The top shelf held "books of so-called Natural Science," from which she did learn at least the names of sundry astronomers, chemists and physicists, whom she forthwith classed with Dr. Priestley and "revered indiscriminately." Walter Scott, "in nine large volumes of bad print," was followed by Shakespeare, Milton, Byron and Goldsmith; long shelves of Bancroft, Prescott and Parkman;

---

[4] *Loc. cit.*

[5] The description of the Fourth Day meetings and the reference to Friend Robert Biddle is from Frances Williams Browin, *A Century of Race Street Meeting House, 1856-1956* (Philadelphia, 1956), pp. 21-23.

and, fortunately near the floor for maturer reflection, Emerson, Channing, Carlyle and Spencer.

Her tenth birthday brought an added delight. She was on the floor of the study lost in a large new book, *The Resources of California*, when her father entered the room. So impressed was he with the fact that text as well as illustrations held her interest, that he immediately "welcomed me with enthusiasm into a companionship which has enriched my whole life."[6]

One can well imagine the pleasure and surprise of this intense, preoccupied public man. William Kelley was strongly attached to his family, as his frequent and often lengthy letters from Washington show. But at home the series of births and tragic deaths were taking their toll of his wife; and young William was apparently more interested in school and sports than politics. So it was Florence who kept her father company in his study or on long walks, and who eagerly listened to and stored away the many things he talked about.

One thought he particularly stressed: it was the duty of his generation to build up America's industries in order to produce enough wealth for the whole country. "The duty of your generation," he continued, "will be to see that the product is justly distributed. The same generation cannot do both"—an injunction so solemnly laid that she could never forget it.[7]

During the next several years her health seems to have improved, while her life remained otherwise uneventful. We get a few brief glimpses of her through her father's letters from the Capital in 1871: in February, "I hope Florrie sustained no permanent injury" (with no further reference to the mishap); in April, "I hope Florrie will enjoy her visit to Germantown." The child must have been a regular and satisfactory correspondent, for on March 12 Congressman Kelley wrote to his wife:

---

[6] *The Survey, op. cit.*, p. 9.

[7] *Ibid.*, p. 8. Cf. John R. Commons: "Her father, the famous Congressman, always said that his generation must establish the Protective tariff to support American industries and the next generation should establish labor legislation to protect American labor and give labor its fair share of what the tariff would make possible." Quoted from a written tribute to Florence Kelley on the occasion of the fortieth anniversary of the National Consumers League, Dec. 9, 1939. NCL files, Library of Congress, Washington, D.C.

"What an admirable letter Florrie writes for one so young and whose health has kept her from school so long!"[8]

Late that summer, following the fifth death among the Kelley children, the family traveled to the Alleghanies, in the heart of the steel producing area, to give the shattered mother a change of scene. The Bessemer process had just been introduced, and Florence's father, always interested in prospects for industrial expansion, took her to watch the "terrifying sight" of a steel pouring.

He had explained in advance how the new process would stimulate both population and industry, thereby "increasing the greatness of this industrial Republic." What he did not discuss, or even seem to notice, was something that attracted Florence's attention immediately—dozens of little boys smaller even than herself, darting about in the fitful light and flaming heat "carrying heavy pails of water and tin dippers" for the perspiring workers. It was two o'clock in the morning, "the first time I had consciously been awake at that hour"; yet to the adults, intent upon this "industrial novelty," the laboring children "were no more important than so many grains of sand in the molds."

Just as disturbing was her visit some weeks later to a glass factory near Pittsburgh, in preparation for which she had been kept in bed the previous twenty-four hours.[9] At midnight she and her father entered the factory. The only light was the glare from the furnaces. In front of each stood a worker with his long blow-pipe. On the floor between worker and furnace, his head almost level with the fiery oven mouth, crouched the "blower's dog," a boy whose function "was to take the blower's mold the instant the bottle or tumbler was removed from it, scrape it and replace it perfectly smooth and clean for the next bottle or tumbler" already being shaped.

No one gave a thought to the amount of heat endured by those small heads at oven height. "The picture of these little figures moving about in the shadows, carrying trays of glass,

---

[8] Letters in the possession of Mr. John B. Kelley, who kindly permitted me to read and quote from them.

[9] *New York Times,* Dec. 7, 1924, Sec. IX, p. 6. The description of this visit is included in Mrs. Kelley's testimony in behalf of the Child Labor Amendment, as reported by the *Times.*

cutting themselves occasionally upon broken glass in the dark, or being burned by the hot bottles" never left her. Young as she then was, she was still uncomfortably aware of being among people for whom the product was everything, the working child nothing. Even her own loved and loving father, unbelievable as it seemed, appeared to count industrial development above "conservation of the human material."

Other trips on two successive summers further widened her horizons. In 1872 the whole family journeyed to the Far West, stopping at Denver, Salt Lake, Los Angeles and Laramie. The trip was a combination of business and pleasure, a part of Congressman Kelley's program of visiting each state and territory during his tenure. The next year Florence traveled with her father and Henry C. Carey over the newly constructed Northern Pacific route, which by then had reached as far as Bismarck, North Dakota.[10]

Her longest uninterrupted attendance at school, six months, began in the fall of 1873, when she was enrolled in a school for girls run by the sisters Mary Anna and Susan Longstreth. There the curriculum for the hundred or so students included sewing, poetry reading, meticulous spelling drill, and "Europe classes," this last based on maps, photographs, guide books and personal recollections of a trip abroad taken by the sisters some twenty years earlier.[11] For Florence, stimulated by her adult associations and her unusual reading range, this must have been feeble fare indeed.

A major turning point in her life came on the day she found "in the otherwise empty wastebasket" in her father's study, "Cornell's offer of equal intellectual opportunity for women," and begged Judge Kelley to let her prepare to meet the entrance requirements. The "offer" is not further identified. It might

---

[10] Congressman Kelley had had a keen interest in a Northern Pacific railroad route from the time he had been approached on the subject by Asa Whitney in the summer of 1845. By December, 1846, Kelley had succeeded in bringing together a group of Philadelphians ready to sponsor the project, and he subsequently spoke in Congress in behalf of a Government bill to aid construction of the railroad. He considered it "chief among the great works of the future . . . which will add inconceivably to the wealth, power and influence of the nation." "The New Northwest," in *Speeches*, etc., *passim.*

[11] Helen Ludlow, *Memoir of Mary Anna Longstreth, with sketch of her work* (Philadelphia, n.d.), *passim.*

have been the one-page "Special Notice to Lady Students" issued in the early seventies, calling attention to "equal privileges in every department of the University." Or perhaps it was the folder listing fifteen "Advantages of Lady Students at Cornell University," including attendance at lectures by such visiting notables as Louis Agassiz, James Russell Lowell, Bayard Taylor and Goldwin Smith; as well as full access to laboratories, draughting rooms, geological and other collections, sermons and religious exercises, and the gymnasium.[12]

Entrance requirements at the time included, besides "a good moral character," political and physical geography, English grammar, arithmetic, physiology, plane geometry, and algebra through quadratic equations. Those who elected Natural History were required in addition to be qualified in plane trigonometry, Latin and Greek.[13]

The admission age of seventeen for women gave her two years in which to make ready. "Careful inquiry soon revealed that there was no school in Philadelphia equipped to fit a girl thoroughly for college." Nor were the "tutors and governesses," eventually located to prepare her, themselves college graduates.

"An excellent verbal memory," and the ability to cram, saw her through her examinations in June, 1876. The rest of the summer was spent between visits to the Centennial Exposition, and preparing to work off leftover conditions in Greek, Latin and algebra. Thus fortified, in September she entered the freshman class, and took up her residence in Sage College.

---

[12] These leaflets are in the Cornell Archives. Lowell delivered two series of twelve lectures each, during the spring terms of 1869 and 1870, too early for Florence Kelley to have heard him.

[13] Cornell *Register* for 1876-77, p. 79.

CHAPTER III

Cornell and the Wider View

The transformation of Cornell University into a coeducational institution was a triumph of idealism, patience and skill. Chartered under the Morrill Land Grant Act in 1865, it had opened its doors three years later to an all-male student body. The limitation was never intended to be other than temporary. The university's principal benefactor, Ezra Cornell, had wished to create an establishment "where any person can find instruction on any subject"; and Andrew D. White, Cornell's first president, had long been convinced that women "might well be admitted to some of the universities for young men."[1]

To almost all of the first board of trustees, coeducation at the university level was wellnigh unthinkable. Of federally-endowed institutions, only a small number in the Midwest were beginning to invite both sexes, none as yet in the East. Moving carefully, White submitted to the board an organizational report that ingenuously substituted the word "person" wherever the word "man" might have been used. The report was approved in that form and the work was launched. In 1870 Henry Sage offered to endow a college for women, and in due time President White was able to report that a majority of the trustees' committee favored Mr. Sage's proposal, including the stipulation that "instruction shall be afforded to young women . . . as broad and as thorough as that now afforded to young men." The recommendations were accepted unani-

---

[1] Carl Becker, *Cornell University, The Founding and the Founders* (New York, 1943), p. 88; *Autobiography of Andrew D. White, op. cit.,* I, 397. With regard to his stand on coeducation, White remarked that his mother "exercised perhaps the strongest influence."

mously, and in the fall of 1874 Sage College enrolled forty-nine young women.[2]

When Florence Kelley entered the freshman class two years later, she found the women students "a serious, self-conscious body of pioneers," who both reveled in and jealously guarded the freedom and equality that had drawn them to Cornell. In general they were hardly more than tolerated by the men students, many of whom, fearing ridicule by other universities, had been actively opposed to the admission of women. At the same time, some of the early women applicants resented the separate lecture rooms, libraries and other facilities of Sage College, along with the "lady wardens who served as guide, philosopher and friend," viewing all this as "a deep conspiracy against women's rights, and insisting that they be treated exactly like young men."[3]

Of immediate importance to Florence, however, was that here before her lay the open road to knowledge. The elective system was exactly tailored to her enthusiasm, and she at once "embarked upon a schedule of twenty-five hours a week" that included French, German, Latin, algebra, literature, natural history and astronomy. In addition, there were the entrance conditions still to be absolved.[4]

It was just the sort of challenge she enjoyed. In excellent health at last, "an-hungered and athirst for learning and for young companionship which now abounded on every side," set down among the seven hills of Ithaca with all the beauty of the changing seasons—to her nothing seemed too difficult or impossible. "Little did we care that there was no music, no theatre, almost no library; that the stairs to the lecture halls were wooden and the classrooms heated with coal stoves."

Yet for all the energies released by their new found opportunities, the Sageites of 1876 exhibited a curious insularity.

---

[2] "Report submitted to the Trustees of Cornell University in behalf of a majority of the Committee on Mr. Sage's Proposal to Endow a College for Women," by Andrew D. White, chairman of the Committee (Albany, Feb. 13, 1872), in the Cornell Archives; *Autobiography of Andrew D. White, op. cit.,* p. 401.

[3] *Ibid.,* pp. 401-402.

[4] Letter from the Office of the Registrar, Cornell University, March 27, 1961. All references to Florence Kelley's curriculum are from this letter. Direct quotation and references to entrance conditions are in "When Co-education Was Young," *The Survey,* Feb. 1, 1927, p. 560.

In 1876

In 1879

Cornell Campus in 1870

Pres. Andrew D. White

Ezra Cornell

No one seems to have read a daily newspaper or subscribed to any of the current periodicals. "I do not believe," wrote Florence Kelley later, "that the New York Nation had one subscriber in Ithaca."[5] The Hayes-Tilden controversy was wracking the whole country, and Congressman Kelley, in New Orleans as an observer at the counting of the votes, had written his daughter of the exciting events; yet, as she recalled, "none of my friends among the students was interested enough to listen to his letters." Outside of the science laboratories there appeared to have been little sustained reading or discussion.

A memorable exception was the small group of young women whom M. Carey Thomas,[6] then a senior, brought together to read Swinburne; and Florence was "deeply impressed" when she was asked to join them. The invitation was conveyed by Ruth Putnam, whose older sister, Dr. Mary Putnam Jacobi, was the first woman to have graduated from the Paris School of Medicine, and whose brother George had several years earlier inherited his father's publishing house. To the friendship established with Carey Thomas and Ruth Putnam was added that of Harriet May Mills, who was to become a leading suffragist, and Frances Mitchell (later Mrs. Hans Froelicher) a fellow Philadelphian; and the five young women were often seen together on the campus lawns or in the college halls.[7]

Cornell's records in those days were sparse, but there is enough in them to show the courses Florence took under the trimester system then in effect. Her schedule was cut to the liberal arts pattern of literature and language courses, her studies in the latter aided by a special aptitude and a fine ear. Beyond that, except for three terms of American history, she elected to sample rather than to concentrate. The sampling was not entirely random. A term each of law, economics and politics suggested the lines along which her interests were beginning to take shape.

[5] *The Survey, op. cit.,* p. 559. It is interesting that two years later the Cornell *Era* would write: "The *Nation* man has begun posting his seductive notices again. A five-weeks subscription should be made compulsory upon the Freshmen by the Faculty and the *Nation* agent should be retired on a pension." Nov. 7, 1878, p. 68.

[6] Within another decade Miss Thomas would become dean of the newly-founded (1885) Bryn Mawr College, and in 1894 its first woman president.

[7] Dr. Hans Froelicher, Jr., of Baltimore, recalls seeing an early photograph of the five friends posed on the college steps.

Her first year passed without untoward incident, but her second was interrupted by an unspecified illness that sent her back to Philadelphia for several weeks. There she found as house guest an acquaintance of her father's who was convalescing after an accident, and whom she helped entertain during his period of recuperation.

"For me," she wrote in the memoirs, "Mr. Livingston was a visitor from Mars." His occupation, importing fine laces, was in itself romantic enough, since it took him abroad several times a year. Moreover, his father had been a friend of Karl Marx, and he himself had recently visited the headquarters of the First International which were then in Hoboken. The pamphlets he had bought there, "printed . . . on cheap paper in bad print and bound in flaming covers," he gave Florence to read. The effect of these "ideas and ideals undreamed of," she recalls, was as startling as her discovery of Aunt Sarah's refusal to use sugar or cotton.

In view of her later commitment, it is a pity that she records nothing further about this incident—the contents of the pamphlets, other conversations, even a stray question or two. We do know that in retrospect she considered the encounter ample compensation for the time lost at Cornell, which would have been spent on "logic, economics, the history of philosophy and the philosophy of history . . . set forth in four small square black books . . . by a superannuated minister who purported to elucidate all four subjects."[8] As a parting gift, Mr. Livingston had presented Florence with a copy of Vasari's *Lives of the Painters,* but, as she wrote, "his abiding influence on my mind was rooted in those fugitive leaflets."[9]

There seems to have been nothing of a socio-political nature at Cornell until the founding of a Social Science Club in the fall of 1878. Literary and fraternal societies were already flourishing on campus, but the Club was the first attempt "to give

---

[8] This unflattering description can only refer to the Reverend William Dexter Wilson (1816-1900), who for Cornell's first eighteen years was the whole philosophy department, as well as registrar for the university. "During his professorship . . . he lectured regularly on psychology, logic, moral philosophy, the history of philosophy and the philosophy of history, and occasionally also on political economy and international law." Waterman Thomas Hewett, *Cornell University, A History* (New York, 1905), II, 66.

[9] "My Novitate," *The Survey,* Apr. 1, 1927, p. 35.

advantages of a more liberal culture to its members than might be gained from the literary societies." On October 30 some twenty invitees, including Florence, met in Association Hall to form an organization whose object was to be "the free and impartial consideration of the live questions of the day, social, moral and political."[10]

The Minutes Book shows her an active participant from the start. The draft constitution laid before the body has her penciled signature heading an appended list of nine names. During the discussion of the draft she moved several amendments intended to enlarge the voice of the membership in the affairs of the society. When the time came for election of officers she received two votes for president, six for vice-president, and was elected secretary unanimously.

The birth of the club had some unexpected consequences. The campus newspaper, the Cornell *Era*, had got wind of the proposed club shortly before the organizational meeting, and ran a paragraph calling attention to a student attempt to organize a "Young Men's Infidel Association."[11] Whether meant as jest or no, it was picked up seriously by the Ithaca *Democrat* (October 31, 1878), which warned that old-fashioned parents "who still believe in a God" would be unwilling "to send their sons and daughters to be educated where infidel associations were allowed," and counseled the college authorities to "nip this organization in the bud."

This the authorities showed no inclination to do; and in this stand they received support and approval both off campus and on. The Ithaca *Journal* wished the new club abundant success, the Cornell *Review* rapped the *Democrat* over the knuckles, and the *Era* sought to make amends by recommending that "every public-spirited scholar" apply for membership.

Despite these endorsements there seems to have been no rush of students into the club; the December *Review* reported that there were now thirty-five members, including Professors Shack-

---

[10] Social Science Club minutes (Cornell archives), p. 30. A preliminary meeting had been held on October 18 in Professor Willard Fiske's room, Number 7 South University. Professor Fiske held the chair of Northern European Languages. The "object of the Club" is found in Article II of the Constitution.

[11] Oct. 25, 1878, p. 55.

ford and Oliver.[12] But for some months at least, meetings took place regularly on a semi-monthly basis, with the Secretary in faithful attendance on her duties. The minutes for December 4 noted that at the first meeting after the holidays there would be "A paper by Miss Kelley on 'National Universities.'"

The paper was never presented. Miss Kelley returned from her vacation with a diphtheria infection, which did not manifest itself until after she had started back to Ithaca. She arrived "in a stupor" and was put to bed in Sage Dormitory. No experienced hospital nurse being available, she was finally supplied with a local nurse, who not only was unaware of the dangers of overdosing, but forgot the doctor's orders to stop medication after ten days. "I received brandy at two hours' intervals, from January to mid-May, following strychina and other poisons. Three years out of college were the penalty . . ."

Although the attack itself was a relatively mild one, the doctor recommended that no attempt be made to move the patient for several months. Florence's older brother William came to stay in Ithaca until she was out of danger, and her closest friend Margaret Hicks was in constant attendance on her.

By April, accompanied by Margaret, she was back in Philadelphia and mending rapidly. In June, when her father left to begin his tour of the Continent, she was well enough to go with him, Margaret and William completing the party. Out of deference to Florence's slowly growing strength they traveled in leisurely fashion through Belgium, Holland and Germany, and ended with several weeks in Paris. The journey, bracketed by the long sea voyages, did her a world of good; but any thought of returning to Cornell was to be put aside for the next several years.[13]

The winter of 1881-1882 she spent in the milder Washington climate, reading law with her father and collecting material at the Library of Congress for a senior thesis. Her topic, "On

---

[12] Charles Chauncey Shackford, professor of rhetoric and oratory, 1871-1886. James Edward Oliver, assistant professor of mathematics, 1871-1873, full professor until his death in 1895. Hewett, *op. cit.*, IV, 16, 57.

[13] WDK to CBK, Jan. 14 and 19, and June 24, 1879; CBK to WDK, April 12, 1879. Letters in possession of the Kelley family.

Some Changes in the Legal Status of the Child Since Blackstone," was formidable enough. Yet the choice reflected an underlying current of emotion. The disposition to examine problems from the standpoint of the law she certainly owed to her father. But beyond that, the early lessons he had impressed upon her, together with her own observation of child workers, had aroused the deep concern that determined the selection of her subject.

In the memoirs she refers to the thesis as "slight enough . . . compared to the scholarly documents of today." Yet with all its limitations it was a piece of research that went far beyond the Bachelor's requirements. In the Library she had painstakingly tracked down "all the authorities on the common and statutory law affecting children; and . . . the official reports of the few state bureaus of labor statistics." The meager American statistics she augmented with data from English records.

Her general finding was that in the century or so since publication of the *Commentaries*, the status of the child had changed as his welfare became the direct object of legislation. From a chattel he had become "an individual possessed of legal status independent of the family." This conclusion she based on evidence in three areas: custody, protection, education; and in each of these she looked at the child within the family (the normal relationship) and without the family (the illegitimate child, the pauper, the juvenile misdemeanant or criminal).

In the first two areas this altered status is illustrated by the shift from the concept of the parent's "vested right" *in* the child to that of the child's right to the custody and protection most wholesome for *him*. His welfare now takes precedence over the claim of either parent; and the general or common law right of the parent to protect his child is transformed into the universal right of the child to be protected. The new concept applies also to the pauper or delinquent child. In Blackstone's time, that unfortunate creature was delivered over to almshouse or jail with the same severity as an adult. In nineteenth century America, on the other hand, the tendency has been to avoid institutionalizing wherever possible.

In the third area, education, she stresses the correlation between legal provisions for education and the extension of suffrage. Where suffrage was severely restricted, as in seventeenth century England, so was state-decreed education. By the nineteenth century, when England had widened suffrage to an extent comparable to that of seventeenth century New England, English compulsory education had attained a level roughly corresponding to that of early America. This leads her to observe that "the removal of the duty of education from the family to the State must receive a decided impulse from every extension of suffrage."

In conclusion, she distinguishes three forces that have contributed to the changed legal status of the child: *economic* (or technological)—the application of steam to machinery, which has given children status as individuals by drawing them into industry; *political*—the extension of suffrage, which compels the State to educate the child as future citizen; and *ethical* or moral—"the growing value attached to human life, and to human personality, and the attendant respect for individuality in every form."[14]

Although her writing is drily factual and often cumbersome, in general she argues straightforwardly from evidence to conclusions. One exception is her handling of the conflict between the needs of the child and a certain set of claimed "rights"— the right of each parent with respect to the other, of both with respect to the child, and reciprocally of the child with respect to his parents and the family structure. It is a worrisome question. She touches on it no less than three times in the course of her paper, only begins to discuss it in the last section, and arrives at no clear solution.

Her initial assumption is that "the child's prime safeguard is the family, and whatsoever strikes the family wounds the child." But protective legislation, by intervening between child and parent, *in fact* "invades" the family. And in setting the child's individual right above the unity of the family, such legislation weakens the very unity which should be the child's "prime safeguard." She is thus left with the paradoxical conclusion that it is "the growing value attached to human life"

---

[14] The ethical factor always occupied an important place in her thinking. It is a theme she returned to almost a quarter of a century later in a full length book, *Some Ethical Gains Through Legislation,* ed. Richard T. Ely (New York, 1905).

which constitutes "perhaps the one dangerous force of all that has been molding infancy legislation."

The error of her argument is a familiar one. Having first absolutized what she later recognized to be a changing institution— the family—she then finds that the very real need for child protection collides with certain abstract rights inherent in the institution as absolutized. This is the kind of error that has been exploited by opponents of protective legislation down to the present day, not only in regard to children but also to all underprivileged or unrepresented groups. It has been used, for example, to conjure up an irreconcilable conflict between wage-hour legislation and freedom of contract, between protective laws for women and equal rights. It is one which Florence Kelley herself was to meet head-on many times in later years and, released from the bonds of unreal abstraction, to combat successfully.

Meanwhile the completed thesis and three more months of classes at Cornell, March to June, 1882, won her the degree of Bachelor of Literature and an Honorable Mention. Her thesis appeared that August in *International Review*, which just the previous March had published an article by her father.[15] There was as yet no Phi Beta Kappa chapter at Cornell, but when one was established the following year she was awarded a key.

Aside from the honors accruing to the young author, the significance of her thesis lies not so much in what it was intended to be, a scholastic labor of duty, as in what it became—the first stage in her development toward the social role she was to play. She had set out to examine a series of statutes and academically to note their changing pattern. But in so doing she had begun to see something of the process whereby social institutions are created and changed, and to understand how those institutions affect and are affected by the men and women and children whose lives and problems were to be her chief concern.

A more direct involvement in some of those problems was soon to come. Following graduation, she had applied for enroll-

---

[15] "A Science Based on Assumptions," pp. 285-98, a discussion of free trade versus protection. *International Review*, A. S. Barnes Co., New York. Bi-monthly 1874-1878; monthly 1879-1883. Eds. (of monthly) Robert P. Porter and Henry Gannett.

ment in the graduate school of the University of Pennsylvania. Her ultimate objective was law school, in preparation for which she wanted to study advanced Greek. After a summer of waiting she was completely taken aback to receive a letter rejecting her application, with the comment by Dr. Horace Furness, the trustee who signed the letter, that "the more he knew people . . . the more abhorrent was the thought of young men and women meeting in the classroom."[16]

Thus denied any immediate prospect of pursuing her studies, she sought another outlet for her energies. She found one at the New Century Club of Philadelphia.[17] A year earlier, in October, 1881, she had been one of a dozen or so young women called together by Mrs. Eliza Sproat Turner, the Club secretary, to discuss setting up evening classes for working women. The project, known as the New Century Working Women's Guild, was a success from the start. As recalled in the Guild's Diamond Anniversary brochure, subjects offered were singing, French and literature, drawing and physiology, German, oral reading, bookkeeping, and history, with Florence Kelley listed as instructor for the last. She does not tell us if she did any teaching that fall before going to Washington with her father. But the memoirs note that in September, 1882, she organized several classes of her own in rooms provided by the club.

As she describes it, most of the students attracted by the Guild at that time were undernourished little girls ranging in age from fourteen to seventeen—"mill hands, domestic servants, dressmakers and shop girls." With pathetic eagerness they flocked into the club until they "overflowed . . . all available space, including stairways and halls." Arithmetic was one subject they all chose, hoping thereby to increase wages that ran as low as a dollar and a half a week. A close second was French, not for any economic advantage but as an "accomplishment."

She must have considered this experience, brief as it was to

---

[16] This is the Dr. Furness who was editor of the *Variorum* edition of Shakespeare. He was a friend of the Kelleys and son of the minister of the church they attended. Mrs. Kelley writes in her memoirs that many years later she learned that the real reason for her rejection was that the University had no course in advanced Greek.

[17] The Club was founded in 1877 "to create an organized centre of thought and action among women, for the protection of their interests and the promotion of science, literature and art . . ." Jane Cunningham Croly, *History of the Woman's Club Movement in America* (Pennsylvania, 1898), p. 1022.

be, both useful and enlightening, for she hastened to set down her thoughts in an article, "Need Our Working Women Despair?", published in *International Review* for November, 1882. A rambling sort of piece, it is worthy of notice as an attempt to indicate remedial measures for certain social ills as she had observed them. The problem was the health and welfare of working women. Her solution tumbles together an assortment of suggestions: from self-help, including regular exercise and suitable work clothing; through "associations of ladies for the legal protection of working women," to a perceptive demand for higher wages based on equality of pay—a demand, she points out, already made vocal by the Knights of Labor.

The Guild classes were her first extended personal contact with workers, and they provided her with the beginnings of a new insight. She had already moved beyond her thesis when she could write: "[T]he facts of . . . human relations must be studied as they exist, with patient care; but exact tabulation of facts is the beginning only; afterward comes the work of interpretation." While her own interpretation may have fallen short at the time, she was already beginning to realize that direct contact with the people behind the statistics provides the indispensable corrective.

This particular contact, unfortunately, was abruptly cut short just before Thanksgiving. William Junior had fallen ill, and was ordered to proceed immediately to the Riviera for a cure. On four days notice only Florence was available to accompany him—William in fact would have no one but his sister—and in four days they were packed and on their way.

CHAPTER IV

The Wider View and Zürich

The journey to the Mediterranean was not very far along when it was halted by a near disaster. The travelers had passed through Liverpool, London and Paris, and by January had reached Avignon. Here William temporarily lost his sight, and they were obliged to remain in the little Provençal town until spring.

It was "a lonely sojourn," as Florence was to recall it. The weather was the worst possible for an invalid, with the cold fierce mistral blowing all winter long. Conversation with the townsfolk was difficult, since the language spoken was much more akin to the ancient *langue d'oc* than to her own fluent French. There was no American consul at Avignon, and no doctor. William's condition required round-the-clock attention; his blindness rendered him almost completely helpless. His sister dared not leave him alone, and even slept in his room at night.

The one bright spot in that "grim, gray experience" was the evening that M. Carey Thomas stopped at the hotel. Miss Thomas, after graduating from Cornell, had gone on to study at Leipzig and Zürich, and had just been awarded a doctorate *summa cum laude* (rare for a man, unheard of for a woman) by the latter university. She was now traveling through Italy and southern France with her friend Mamie Gwinn, and was on her way to London for the Rossetti exhibition.

The three young women "sat at a little round table during dinner," and as Miss Thomas told of her experiences Florence found her own hopes rekindled.[1] She had already considered applying to Oxford after her rejection by the University of

---

[1] *The Survey, op. cit.*, p. 601; letter from M. Carey Thomas to her mother, London, Jan. 13, 1883, in NCL files, Library of Congress.

Pennsylvania the summer before; now Zürich and Germany seemed to open up new and exhilarating possibilities.

Careful nursing into the spring effectually restored William's sight and health. In April Miss Thomas met them again, this time in Paris, and described the meeting in a letter to her mother:

> Miss Kelley dined with me yesterday and I had a charming talk. She has done a great deal of good in a philanthropic way, starting tenement houses [*sic!*] etc., in Phila. Her legal thesis at Cornell was passed very highly. She amounts to more than any other Cornell men or girls except my Miss Clements. . . . Their mother arrives at Liverpool on the 1st of May and they are going to meet her.[2]

By early June the whole family had gathered again in London. Here they were joined by Congressman Kelley not yet fully recovered from his operation. And here, having heard of her old friend's illness, Miss Anthony came to call one Sunday afternoon, with her young secretary and companion, Rachel Foster.[3]

As the summer wore on, the elder Kelley's health improved enough for a journey through the English Midlands with his daughter. In Manchester they called upon United States consul Albert D. Shaw, where the conversation turned to economic comparisons between America and England, and dwelt in particular on the tariff question.

The Congressman had an easy formula: free admission of goods not produced at home, and a high tariff on all other imports to prevent undercutting by "the pauper labor of Europe." He was therefore greatly surprised when Consul Shaw began to speak of the stimulating effect of free competition on the English textile industry. Forced to install the most up-to-date machinery to meet the competition of the French and German markets, Shaw pointed out, English manufacturers

---

[2] Letter from Miss Thomas to her mother, April, 1883. This letter and the preceding one were copied from the originals by Miss Thomas' biographer, Edith Finch, for Josephine Goldmark, and are among Miss Goldmark's papers in the NCL files. Miss Clements is the Gabrielle Clements (B.S. Cornell, '80) listed as having taught "drawing and physiology" at the New Century Working Woman's Guild in 1881.

[3] The Misses Anthony and Foster were in London during a suffrage speaking tour. Miss Anthony refers to her visit to the Kelleys in a letter to her sister dated June 22, 1883. Harper, *op. cit.*, II, 564.

WILLIAM DARRAH KELLEY, JR.

At about 17

As a young man

ALBERT BARTRAM KELLEY

As a little boy

As a young man

A view of Zürich and the River Limmat

were able not only to put out an improved product, but to do so with a shorter work week than American mills and no real difference in wages. In contrast, said the Consul, the high American tariff walls, by providing a privileged sanctuary for obsolescent equipment, were largely responsible for the backward state of the American cotton industry. To the young woman brought up under a high tariff philosophy these were challenging ideas, and they began to raise some disquieting doubts.

As the conversation took a different turn, she was further impressed by the Consul's extensive discussion of protective laws for English wage earners. Remembering the long hours of searching for her thesis material, she welcomed the opportunity to learn from Mr. Shaw "more than I could have gathered from a dozen volumes."

The legislative protection they talked about, however, did not extend to the nail and chain makers the Kelleys saw at a later stage in their journey. Scattered through the Black Country in miserable little huts, these workers suffered from exploitation of the rankest kind, as bad as the sweatshop system Florence Kelley was to encounter time and again in her own country. It was always to be a source of distress to her that attempts to relieve worker exploitation could so easily be sidetracked by starting an argument over the tariff question. Tariff or no, she had seen it repeatedly demonstrated that the only way to improve working conditions was to pass legislation specifically for that purpose. Indeed, as she wrote in 1927, recalling her Midlands journey, the existence of the "sweating system" in both free trade England and protectionist America showed that "the old debate between free trade and protective tariff . . . so far as it hinged on overwork and underpay of workers at the bottom level of industry, was . . . unreal."

But in 1883, in spite of the questions raised by Consul Shaw's reasoning, the case for a protective tariff still seemed the more cogent, particularly in light of the poverty she had just witnessed. Eager to record her impressions while they were fresh, she wrote a series of letters describing what she had seen, and attributing the plight of the English working people to the English system of free trade. She sent the manuscript on to

still standing there as the train pulled out. Nor did she ever see it again.

Fearing that she would not be admitted without the diploma, she detailed her plight to Herr Pedell, dean of the Zürich Polytechnikum. He heard her out, "immobile as any beadle celebrated by Dickens," then dismissed her loss as of no consequence, since "an American diploma has no value." Relieved that there were no further obstacles, on October 13 she enrolled as a student.

Houghton Mifflin and Company, who at the time accepted it for publication.

During that summer, too, she finally reached the decision to pursue her graduate studies at the University of Zürich. Earlier she had gone up to Oxford, but "found little offered to an American woman student." In September she set out for Switzerland with her mother and younger brother, where Albert was to attend school while she herself entered the University.

One anxiety still beset her. On the way back from Oxford she had lost her trunk containing her Cornell diploma. For no apparent reason the trunk had been taken off the train at Rugby Junction, and in spite of her pleas to the guard it was

The city that she had come to was very old and very beautiful, with steep narrow streets winding upward, and many bridges spanning the river Limmat that flowed through its heart. Upon the Abbey, the ancient cathedral, the guildhouses lining the water's edge, a thousand years of history had set their mark.

Much less ancient was the University, built on high ground and overlooking the city. Founded in 1832 as a cantonal institution, it soon began to attract students not only from all of Switzerland but from other countries as well. In 1855 the Polytechnikum was opened, and for a number of years the two institutions shared professors, including such renowned teachers and lecturers as Johann Bluntschli, Theodor Mommsen, Friedrich Lange and Richard Avenarius.[4]

Initially, the question of admitting women did not arise, but in 1864 a Russian woman asked for and received permission

[4] Dr. Willy Spühler, 100 *Jahre Universität Zürich*, (Zürich, 1932), pp. 2-4.

to audit courses in natural science. Two years later she was followed by another; and in 1867 the senate of the University, "quietly but well knowing what they were doing," decided as a matter of principle to welcome women students on an equal basis with men.[5] The first European university to do so, Zürich thus became a focal point for women who wished to study especially law and medicine, and who were barred in their own countries by statute, as in Russia, or by prejudice, as in so many other places.

On first acquaintance the Polytechnikum must have seemed austere compared to American or to other European universities. There were no fraternities or sororities, no athletics, no boatraces though Lake Zürich beckoned, not even any dormitories. But adequate lodging was to be found in the many pensions scattered through the city; and for recreation there was much music and a small and charming repertory theatre.

Her year and a half since graduation had given Florence Kelley a clearer perspective on how best to equip herself for the future. Her sampling days had been ended by the discipline of her bachelor's thesis, and her choice of specialization had been made. But her encounters of the past summer in particular had shown her that the study of law in and for itself was not enough. She must make of her profession not simply a practice but a tool, a defense, a remedy. At the same time she had become increasingly aware that the human conditions so painful to her were deeply rooted in both economic and historical circumstances. This awareness found its reflection in the courses she selected for her first semester—Contemporary History Since 1852, with Professor Gerold Meyer von Knonau; and, with the liberal economist Professor Julius Platter, Theoretical Economics, Political Science, and Communist Ideas and Movements to 1848.[6]

As she noted in the memoirs, her past experiences were scarcely enough to have directed her to socialism as an answer

---

[5] Dr. J. M. Meijer, *Knowledge and Revolution, The Russian Colony in Zuerich, 1870-1873,* Publications on Social History, Internationaal Instituut voor Sociale Geschiednis (Amsterdam, Assen, 1956), pp. 64-67.

[6] Information on Florence Kelley's curriculum is contained in a letter from the Office of the Registrar, University of Zürich, March 6, 1961. She was a registered student at the Polytechnikum from October 13, 1883, to November 30, 1885.

to the questions posed by the social system. There had been her brief introduction to Mr. Livingston and his pamphlets; and a single lecture at Cornell by President White, in which he offered his own quaint and thoroughly garbled "explanation" of socialism to an audience "so unsophisticated . . . that not one question was asked."

But in Zürich the situation was excitingly different. Switzerland had long provided a haven for Europe's politically displaced, and after the passage of Bismarck's "Socialist Law" in 1878 Zürich became a refuge for the ousted German Social Democrats. They had set up headquarters in the city and were publishing a newspaper, the *Sozialdemokrat,* which was being smuggled over the border in defiance of the law. Party meetings were held regularly. Closed sessions alternated with those open to the public, and both were addressed by members of the Executive Committee and editors of the paper.[7]

At the University the atmosphere was one of intense discussion. Many of the students had come there to mend educational careers broken up by the police of their respective countries, and to carry on as best they could the socialist activities for which they had been harried from home. It was both disturbing and inspiring to meet and talk with men and women who had risked their livelihood and often their lives for the sake of the new philosophy. Two of these, unnamed, made a vivid enough impression to find their way into the memoirs forty years later.

One was "a Russian exile, a student of chemistry, who translated Marx, put his manuscript into a small trunk," and set out for his homeland. At Freiburg-im-Breisgau, Germany, he was betrayed and turned over to the Russian police. The Russian government kept him for several years in Peter Paul fortress, and then sent him on to Siberia. Escaping, he made his way via Behring Strait to America, and "found work as a chemist in the Board of Health of a city in the Middle West

---

[7] Eduard Bernstein, *My Years of Exile* (London, 1921), pp. 54-55. As Bernstein notes, a fuller account of the founding of the *Sozialdemokrat* appears in August Bebel, *Aus Meinem Leben* (Stuttgart, 1914), III, 65-67. Bebel gives the date of the first number as 28 September, 1879, but the masthead of Number 1 shows the date October 5. The paper regularly carried notices of party meetings, both open and closed. On film, Columbia University Microfilm Library.

where . . . I was astonished to meet him in the course of my duties as chief factory inspector, in Illinois in the 'nineties.' "[8]

The other, ". . . Viennese, a man of brilliant gifts . . . illegitimate son of a noble at the court of Franz Josef," was undoubtedly Emil Kaler-Reinthal. Considered "the best leader of the Austrian Social Democrats from 1874 to the appearance of Viktor Adler," Kaler-Reinthal supplemented a small government pension by writing for the Socialist press. He had been arrested many times by the Austrian police, until he made his way to safety over the Swiss border, where he continued to function as a Social Democratic leader in Zürich, speaking at party meetings and writing an occasional article for *Die Neue Zeit*. "A highly nervous, over-sensitive man," as Eduard Bernstein described him, he finally committed suicide in 1897.[9]

It may have been in company with such as these that Florence Kelley went to her first Socialist meeting on December 8, 1883, to hear Bernstein, exiled editor of the *Sozialdemokrat*. The meeting was held on the second floor of the Café Kessler in Stüssihofstatt (an old part of the city), a favorite rendezvous for the Social Democrats. The room was well filled. There were perhaps twenty students from a dozen countries, a somewhat larger number of skilled textile and railroad workers, both men and women, from the immediate vicinity, and several leaders of the German Socialist Party in addition to Bernstein. "And here I was in the World of the Future!" she wrote in the memoirs. "I was so trembling with excitement that I grasped the sides of my chair and held them firmly."[10]

The topic announced was "The Program of Social Democracy." Bernstein undertook, in the light of that program, to

[8] "My Novitiate," *The Survey*, Apr. 1, 1927, p. 34. Mrs. Kelley's account raises some questions. The dramatic events she relates tally with those in the autobiography of the Russian revolutionist, Leo Deutsch, *Sixteen Years in Siberia*, tr. Helen Chisholm (London, 1903), except for one fatal discrepancy—Deutsch did not escape from Siberia until 1901. Mrs. Kelley was chief state factory inspector in Illinois for the years 1893-1897. Could she in her memoirs have confused another "Züricher" whom she met in the mid-west in the nineties with the Deutsch she may also have known in Zürich in the eighties?

[9] *The Survey, loc. cit.* Karl Kautsky, *Erinnerungen und Erörterungen* ('s-Gravenhage, 1960), pp. 232, 327; Friederich Engels, *Briefe an Bernstein* (Berlin, 1925), p. 127n (notes by Bernstein). See also Ludwig Brügel, *Geschichte der Oesterreichische Sozialdemokratie* (Vienna, 1922-25), III, *passim*.

[10] *The Survey, op. cit.*, p. 35. Advance announcement of this meeting appeared in *Der Sozialdemokrat* on Dec. 6, 1883.

present an analysis of Bismarck's proposed high tariff. The floor was then thrown open for discussion. The participants covered every aspect Florence Kelley had ever heard or read of, "plus one that was entirely new to me"—the international obligation of workers to their fellows everywhere. Thus, a tariff which raised the living standards of one group should not be the means of depressing the living standards for others, though the latter might be half a world away. (The case in point concerned the silk workers of China and Japan who would be hurt by a high silk import duty in Germany.) How could any arguments for protection, even as carefully reasoned as those of her father and his friend Carey, stand against such a simple concept? "This might well have been a Quaker meeting. Here was the Golden Rule! Here was Grandaunt Sarah!"

Such exuberant acceptance of the philosophy of socialism was less an act of impulse than one of recognition. Florence Kelley's early life and thought had been largely shaped by the pervasive influence of her father and of Aunt Sarah. In their separate ways they had invited her questions and offered answers that at the time had satisfied her. Yet profoundly attached to these two people as she still was, she had begun to sense some very real inadequacies in their outlook.

The ethical humanitarianism that Sarah Pugh represented had served well enough in the simpler society of a pre-Civil War America. There had been time and scope for the exercise of concern for the individual, for the relief of individual distress. On a broader scale, yet still within the framework of Quaker concern, the issues of abolition and of the franchise for women had exerted a strong appeal. But the surge of industrial development after the war created a new situation. It was not easy to hear "the voice of the spirit" above the perpetual clatter of machinery, or see the light of brotherhood through the dense clouds of factory smoke.

The doctrines held by William Kelley exhibited even graver deficiencies. Although he too had taught concern for others, his was a solicitude rooted in *noblesse oblige*, the responsibility of the successful for the less fortunate. Dedicated to progress, he had welcomed industrialization as the necessary instrumentality for the creation of national wealth and perforce well-being. What he did not see—perhaps did not want to see—and what had troubled his daughter even as a little girl, was the enormous price in human suffering exacted by the manner in which industrialization was proceeding. To assure her, as he did, that the proper course was for his generation to produce and for hers to distribute, was only to evade the problem. For under the given conditions of the industrial process, the inevitable result would always be the simultaneous production of both wealth and misery.

It was never any part of Florence Kelley's thought that the answer lay in abandoning industrialization. But she could no longer accept her father's assurance that the market place, left to itself, would even belatedly extend the accrued benefits of economic advance to all the people.

The problem of progress and poverty, as she now saw it, only Marxian socialism could solve. With the major instruments of production owned and controlled by society as a whole, the tremendous energies released by the new industrialization would be employed for the benefit of everyone rather than for the favored few. The same generation would, because it now could, both produce and distribute on an ever-increasing scale, and the Golden Rule of the brotherhood of all mankind, in its fullest sense, would at last be realized.

Here was the promise, the assurance, she had been looking for. It accorded with her vigorous nature to take "the eager plunge into the enthusiasm of the new movement that was beginning to kindle throughout all Europe." Now more than ever was it important to get on with her studies, to fit herself as quickly as possible for the great work that lay ahead.

CHAPTER V

The Socialist Commitment

When Florence Kelley joined the Socialist Party in Zürich in 1884, she did so without any "mental reservations." This she made clear in a letter to Mrs. Carrie Chapman Catt in 1927, shortly after the last of the memoirs had appeared.[1] Mrs. Kelley was at that time under severe attack as a "Red" by the Daughters of the American Revolution, and Mrs. Catt was drafting a scathing reply in the form of "An Open Letter to the D.A.R."[2] Mrs. Kelley wrote that while she had never been "either a Bolshevist or a Communist," she had no intention of repudiating or glossing over her youthful step—a position wholly consonant with her lifelong habit of acting upon conviction and standing by her actions.

We may therefore conclude that matters other than political are responsible for an unexpected gap in the memoirs. The third section breaks off abruptly in 1884, while the fourth and last begins "on a snowy winter morning between Christmas 1891 and New Years 1892," with Florence Kelley standing on the steps of Hull House in Chicago.[3] The intervening period—in-

[1] Letter to Mrs. Carrie Chapman Catt, June 4, 1927, NCL files, Washington, D.C. The full sentence reads: "The Socialist Party, when I joined it in Switzerland in 1884, was a revolutionary party, and I made no mental reservations in joining it."

[2] The D.A.R. were circulating a scurrilous pamphlet attacking Mrs. Kelley and the National Consumers League, Jane Addams and the Women's International League for Peace and Freedom, and Rose Schneiderman and the Women's Trade Union League. The pamphlet was based on a "Petition" drawn up the year before by an organization calling itself the Woman's Patriot Party, Inc., and had been read into the Congressional Record by Senator Bayard of Delaware on July 3, 1926. This was at a time when the Children's Bureau and the Sheppard-Towner Bill were under heavy fire. In a letter to Mrs. Kelley a few days later (June 11), Mrs. Catt wrote: "I think the aim may be to break up women's organizations or at least to break up the Washington lobby and to discredit any influence they may have there." NCL files.

[3] "I Go to Work," *The Survey,* June 1, 1927, p. 271.

43

cluding her marriage, the birth of a son, and five years residence in New York—is dismissed in a single short paragraph.

Her reticence is not difficult to explain. The marriage, begun with such high expectations, lasted but a few years and ended in divorce. Thereafter, as noted by her friend, colleague and biographer Josephine Goldmark, the years passed over in the memoirs remained "a sealed chapter."[4] To that chapter Miss Goldmark herself adds only a few details.

It is now possible, however, to recover much of this missing portion of Florence Kelley's life. A substantial collection of her letters, covering the years 1884 to 1894, has recently become available.[5] Addressed to Friedrich Engels in England, and written from Zürich, New York and Chicago, the correspondence began when she undertook to translate one of Engels' early works. (His side of the correspondence is published in *Letters to Americans, 1848-1895*.)[6] Her first letter is dated December 5, 1884, and thus the correspondence provides a contemporary record that takes up where the memoirs leave off.

Having whole-heartedly embraced the new movement, her first question was how to be of most use while keeping on with her university schedule. During the winter of 1883-84 she had read Marx's *Das Kapital* and sundry works of Engels in the original German—none had as yet appeared in English—and was impressed by what seemed to her their logic and their special value for the American working class. The translation of Volume One of *Das Kapital* (in the hands of Sam Moore and Edward Aveling) was nearing completion at the time, but no

---

[4] Goldmark, *op. cit.*, p. 18.

[5] From Archiv, IML, Fond I, Opis 5. (Archive, Institute of Marxism-Leninism, Fund I, Schedule 5.) The forty letters on microfilm were forwarded by Prof. G. Obichkin, Director, Institute of Marxism-Lennism, Moscow, and were received November 22, 1961. All letters designated "FKW to FE" are from this source.

A few of these letters have also been used in *Aus der Geschichte des Kampfes von Marx und Engels für die proletarische Partei* (Dietz Verlag Berlin, 1961), a collection of essays by a group of Russian authors, published in Moscow in 1955. The last article, by A. A. Poltayev, "Marx und Engels über die Arbeiterbewegung in den USA in den 70er-90er Jahren des 19. Jahrhunderts," quotes briefly from four or five of Florence Kelley-Wischnewetzky's letters to Engels. I came across the collection some time after the original preparation of this manuscript.

[6] International Publishers (New York, 1953), ed. Alexander Trachtenberg, tr. Leonard E. Mins. Engels' letters to Mrs. Florence Kelley-Wischnewetzky were written in English.

one had as yet essayed any of Engels' works. She could make her most immediate contribution, she thought, if she were to take on that task herself.

It was about this time that she fell deeply in love with a fellow student, a Russian socialist, whom she met in her Political Economy lecture course. Lazare Wischnewetzky was soon bringing her material from "a private library of rare books" to which he had access; and on New Year's Day, as Florence wrote her father (Jan. 2, 1884), he paid his first formal call upon her and her mother and brother. A native of Taganrog, he had matriculated in the Medical School in 1880.[7] A contemporary photograph shows a robust young man with a frank, cheerful face, close-cropped curly hair and an air of great charm.[8]

Strongly drawn to him as she was, Florence Kelley nonetheless realized the great gulf of background and outlook that separated them. Lazare Wischnewetzky was dedicated to the revolutionary movement; she had accepted unequivocally the ideals of the movement, but her ideas of service in its behalf were far different from his. From Italy, where she had gone to spend the spring (1884) vacation, she wrote him that to stay in Europe and work at and for Socialism was utterly preposterous and out of the question, and that she could not possibly think of marrying him.[9]

But the ferment, both romantic and political, was at work. Within a few months all seeming obstacles had vanished, and on June 1 they were married.

The union was approved by Caroline Kelley, who from Zürich assured her husband (June 24, 1884): "I can hardly imagine two more congenial spirits." In Philadelphia circles the marriage naturally caused some surprise. Frances Mitchell, studying in Zürich for a doctorate in German philology, had written of it to her younger sister, Mary Virginia, who replied:

---

[7] Letter from the Office of the Registrar, University of Zürich, Mar. 23, 1962. Wischnewetzky was registered in the School of Medicine for the year 1880-81. He attended a clinic in Heidelberg during the winter of 1884-85, and received his doctorate from the University of Würzberg in 1886.

[8] Photograph in the possession of Mr. John B. Kelley. A brief account of the marriage is in Goldmark, *op. cit.*, pp. 17-18.

[9] This is related in a letter, Mar. 19, 1885, from Florence Kelley to Mary Thorn Lewis (later Mrs. William Channing Gannett) of Philadelphia. Five letters to Miss Lewis, dated Jan. 4, Feb. 12, Mar. 19, June 10 and June 22, 1885, have just come to light (Spring, 1964). Letters in possession of the Kelley family.

The part about Florence is very interesting . . . was thee surprised at F. Kelley's engagement. I was so sorry to hear it on thy account for I feared thee would have nobody— it is hard as it is but she will start thee.[10]

At the time, the marriage might well have provided an ideal example for young and serious-minded lovers, resting as it did on "ever deepening respect and ever more intense absorption in work in common and effort for a righteous cause." Now the idea of living and working on the Continent seemed more plausible ("we shall hardly go to America in the near future," she wrote Mary Lewis); and there was even the thought, expressed later to Miss Lewis, of taking on a "foreign correspondenceship of an American paper."[11]

While her new husband continued his medical studies, Florence Kelley herself was carrying a heavy summer schedule— fourteen hours of lectures in law and economics, including three hours a week with the eminent legal scholar Aloys von Orelli o' the philosophy of law. With all the reading entailed, this wou,d have been a full enough program; but there were also the translations she had determined on.

She elected to begin with Engels' *Die Lage der arbeitenden Klasse in England*. She had made a careful study of the work during the previous winter, and by mid-summer was ready to seek the author's permission to translate it for American publication.

Evidently hesitant at approaching the great man directly, she asked Hermann Schlüter, publications manager of the weekly *Sozialdemokrat*,[12] to convey her request for permission to translate *Die Lage*. Schlüter did so, and in August reported that Engels was not only willing for her to go ahead, but that he would write a new preface for the American edition provided she first found a publisher. She of course was delighted, but be-

---

[10] Letter, dated Oct. 26, 1884, in the possession of Dr. Hans Froelicher, Jr. Mary V. Mitchell was at that time resident physician at a Boston hospital. Her sisterly prophecy was soon fulfilled when Frances Mitchell met Hans Froelicher as a fellow student at the University of Zürich. After both had achieved their doctorates *cum laude* they left Switzerland for America, were married in Baltimore and joined the faculty of Goucher College.

[11] FKW to MTL: Jan. 4, 1885; Mar. 19, 1885.

[12] An active member of the German Social Democratic party, Schlüter had, along with his managerial duties, been assigned to establish the archives of the Party in Switzerland. See F. Engels, *Briefe an Bernstein, op. cit.*, p. 175.

Seated, left to right: Caroline B. Kelley, Albert Kelley, Florence Kelley-Wischnewetzky. Standing: Lazare Wischnewetzky

Nicholas Kelley, aged about 1 year

Friedrich Engels   *Karl Marx*

cause of a "tedious illness" was unable to begin work until November.

By then she and her husband were in Heidelberg. They had postponed a honeymoon until after the summer session; and some while later had set off on a leisurely journey that ended, in October, in a pleasant little pension at Theaterstrasse 9. During this time she had become pregnant, and so was glad to settle down to the "quiet student life" offered by the next six months. A letter to Mary Lewis described a typical day:

> My husband vanishes to his first clinic at nine, and is gone three hours, during which I translate or read for my degree. Then we have an hour among the English, American and German papers in the Museum. Then dinner at an admirable club in the neighborhood and a two hours' chat or quiet reading time, over our coffee, in our sunny study. Then come lectures from four until half past seven, during which I again translate or read for my degree. Then tea in the study, and a long evening of reading aloud, rarely the theatre or a concert for we are happier together in our nook. Every day my Mother who, with Albert is in a German pension around two corners from us, comes to me or I go to her. Last night a great exception—we were all lookers on at a carnival maskball in the Museum until midnight.[13]

Once begun, the work on *Die Lage* went well. Early in December she wrote her first letter to Engels, enclosing her translation of the preface and the introduction, a request for any improvements he might suggest, and a short list of German technical terms for which her dictionary and thesaurus had no equivalents.

> Mr. Schlüter tells me (*she continued*) that you are willing to write an English preface for the American edition of the book, but only on condition of my first finding a publisher. I have very little doubt of finding a publisher; but I am much afraid that none will bind himself to publish

---

[13] FKW to MTL, Feb. 12, 1885. Later biographical sketches of Florence Kelley note that she "studied law" at Heidelberg. There is no record at the University of any classes she might have attended, since women matriculants were not admitted until 1900. Before that it was only possible for women to sit in on classes by private arrangement with the lecturer. (Letter from Dr. Hans Krabusch, Universitäts-Archiv, Heidelberg, Oct. 20, 1961.) The letters to Mary Lewis, however, make no reference to such attendance. Although continuing her studies, Florence Kelley, for whatever reason, never did present herself for a degree in law at Zürich.

unless he had the whole, preface included, given him for
inspection. I shall enter at once into correspondence about
the publication and shall of course inform you at once upon
securing a favorable answer. I think it would be especially
fortunate if "die Lage" could appear not very long after
the English translation of "das Kapital."

It seems to me most important that the best of the German socialist literature should be made accessible to my
countrymen in the near future; and, if I should succeed
in making a translation of this first one which should prove
satisfactory to you, I should go on with the work—with
your permission—beginning with the Entwicklung des
Socialismus, taking next der Ursprung der Familie and so
on, finishing with Dührings Umwälzung der Wissenschaft.[14]

Engels seems to have been mildly surprised, though pleased
enough, at the sudden interest in a work that had lain half-
forgotten for almost forty years. He returned her draft with
"some corrections and suggestions in pencil," promised her the
English preface "when things are a little more advanced," and
courteously declined to commit himself for the present on any
further translations.[15]

Her next letter was also from Heidelberg:

I thank you very much for your kind note and correc-
tions just received. . . . I shall gladly avail myself of your
permission to turn to you for English technical equivalents.
It was a relief to me that you propose the omission of the
German preface. An English preface of modern date would,
I think, meet the doubt expressed in the enclosed letter
from the publisher whom I addressed on the subject. Mr.
Putnam is an old friend of mine, and senior partner of
G. P. Putnam's Sons. G. P. Putnam, founder of the firm,
was proprietor of the Putnam's Monthly Magazine, for
which, I think, Karl Marx was a contributor. The high
standing of the firm makes it desirable to secure such an
introduction to American readers, and there is a chance
then for further translations, should they accept this first
one. I shall therefore act upon this suggestion and send
Mr. Putnam the first chapters and a schedule.

I did not mean to take your writings bodily into possession, as my proposition perhaps seems to indicate; but
only to offer my work if no one else were available and in

---

[14] FKW to FE, Dec. 5, 1884.
[15] FE to FKW, Feb. 4, 1885. Unpublished letter, Friedrich A. Sorge Collection,
Manuscript Division, New York Public Library.

case you should be satisfied with my translation of this first one. My one wish is to see such books as Mr. Gronlund's and Professor Ely's supplanted by scientific works, and the more translators the more speedily this result may be attained.[16]

Her hopes that the Putnam firm would take the book were not realized. In spite of the new preface—and the fact, as Engels pointed out, that industrial America in 1885 resembled in many respects the industrial England of 1844[17]—George Putnam felt that the work was outdated, and after temporizing for half the summer, declined to publish it.

In her letters to Mary Lewis during these months, Florence Kelley lost no opportunity to communicate her new social vision, with an air of authority that brooked almost no argument. She found in "every American paper . . . tidings of the coming revolution which you, living among the volcanoes, do not recognize as such . . ." To the charge that she was "one-sided" she agreed, but replied that her friend was "other-sided," hampered like her compatriots by the "excessive poverty of the Anglo-American literature," in contrast to the advanced discoveries of the modern German economists. She herself had written an essay "under the innocent title American Women Students in Zürich," in which she took to task the American economists for their unscientific views, as well as the "so-called intelligent classes" for their "culpable passivity" in the face of daily capitalist assaults on the working class. The essay had made the rounds of the most prominent publications—*North American Review, Popular Science Monthly, Harper's,* the *Woman's Journal*—but was rejected by all of them.

---

[16] FKW to FE, Feb. 6, 1885. The mention of Marx as a contributor to *Putnam's Monthly Magazine* refers to a series of three articles entitled "The Armies of Europe," which appeared in 1855 in the September, October and December issues. Charles Dana, editor of the *New York Daily Tribune*, had asked him to do the articles for Putnam. Marx, overburdened with commitments at the time, turned his material over to Engels for the actual writing. See *Marx Engels Werke,* Dietz Verlag (Berlin, 1961), Vol. XI, note 224, p. 675. The articles were unsigned.

Laurence Gronlund (1846-1901), Danish-American Socialist and member of the Executive Committee of the Socialistic Labor Party, author of *The Cooperative Commonwealth* (1884).

Richard T. Ely (1854-1943), teacher of political economy at Johns Hopkins University and author of *Socialism in France and Germany* (Baltimore, 1883).

[17] FE to FKW, Feb. 10, 1885. *Letters to Americans,* p. 145. Unless otherwise noted, all subsequent letters from Engels to Mrs. Florence Kelley-Wischnewetzky are from this source.

This correspondence also reveals that a serious rift had developed between Florence Kelley and her father, over the letters she had written while traveling with him in England. Houghton Mifflin had delayed publishing them for nearly a year, ("to bring them out before the election [of 1884] as I learned later," she wrote Miss Lewis,) and in the meantime she "outgrew" the views on which the letters had been based. When she found that the book "could be used for advocating Mr. Blaine and Protection and I believe in neither," she composed a supplementary letter explaining her new position. The firm refused the additional letter, and she cancelled the enterprise. "My Father wanted the book for campaign purposes," she added, "and has made my suppression of it—in spite of my elaborate explanations that I could not publish what I no longer believed in—the cause of profound unhappiness for four months past." Even more disturbing was the publicity attendant upon the cancellation: "The whole American and America-European press has published a rumor that Lazare forbade me to publish the poor little worthless book for fear of the Russian authorities(!) whence we became unhappy and I had left him to return to my family!"[18] Judge Kelley, his daughter told Miss Lewis, had sharply and publicly repudiated the "slander"; but the complete divergence in political views between father and daughter became a barrier that almost destroyed the old relationship.

In May the Wischnewetzkys returned to Zürich to await the birth of the baby. "I have been perfectly well ever since the middle of January," she wrote Mary Lewis on June 10, "working six to eight hours daily at translation, dissertation and newspaper correspondence, and I have not the slightest anxiety for the coming time." Her chief care was to finish the translation before the "grand interruption." She had hoped for a boy, and her wish was granted when Nicholas was born on July 12, 1885.

Her work on *Die Lage* completed, there still remained the question of a publisher. She had thought of having the translation brought out in London, after it became clear that George Putnam's negative decision was final; but the idea was dis-

---

[18] FKW to MTL, Mar. 19, 1885.

carded when a new possibility opened up near the end of the year. "A friend of mine," she wrote Engels on December 28, "who has gone to America for two months, has undertaken to find a publisher for the translation of 'die Lage' and, if necessary, to bear the entire cost of the edition."

In this letter she threw some additional light on the Putnam refusal; and also noted the prevailing belief of Americans that their country was an exception to the "rules" of economics:

> I think most of the readers of the translation will say as I did myself, and as Mr. Putnam did: "But the Factory Acts, compulsory education, coöperation and trades unions organizations have done much to remove the evils here described, and the new enfranchisement must do still more," And then, too, all Americans almost without exception, I think, regard America as exempt from the workings of the economic laws which, as they are perfectly willing to acknowledge, manifest themselves elsewhere.

Commenting on her reference to American economic optimism, and carrying the discussion a step further, Engels wrote on January 7, 1886:

> . . . As to those wise Americans who think their country exempt from the consequences of fully expanded capitalist production, they seem to live in blissful ignorance of the fact that sundry states, Massachusetts, New Jersey, Pennsylvania, Ohio, etc., have such an institution as a Labor Bureau, from the reports of which they might learn something to the contrary.

The remark about Labor Bureaus touched a tender spot. A major difficulty in preparing her Bachelor's thesis had been the very meager and incomplete American statistics available, in those states where they were kept at all. In later years her insistent demand would be in no small way responsible for an improved system of record gathering and keeping. Now, it seemed to her, that while what Engels said was true, the value of even those sparse figures was nullified by the misuse to which they were often put. As she wrote in reply on January 10:

> As to the American belief that America is economically "not as other men," it is unfortunately true that the reports of the Statistical Bureaus of Labor have been favorite sources from which the politicians of both the old parties have drawn material by skillful perversions of which

they have persuaded the workingmen of the correctness of their assertion. And that great masses of workingmen believe today in this exemption, our comrades who are most active among them will, I am sure, agree with me in asserting.

She also expressed her gratification that Engels would lose no time in going over the manuscript, as she had just received an urgent letter from her "friend in America." The friend was Rachel Foster,

> the very active secretary of the National Woman Suffrage Association, [who] will see to it that the book is placed in all the many libraries of the assn. and so within reach of a very large body of young workingwomen, teachers etc. . . . Miss Foster is ready, too, to go on publishing Socialist works as fast as I translate them.[19]

The enthusiasm displayed by Miss Foster seems to have mirrored a growing tendency in the America of the eighties— the willingness of a number of those engaged in social protest to accord a respectful hearing to the socialist idea, if not the socialist organization. This was true not only of some sections of the labor movement, but also of various reform groups that drew much of their membership from the middle class. It was the kind of response that would express itself near the end of the decade in the acclaim given Edward Bellamy's *Looking Backward,* and in the formation of the network of Nationalist Clubs that enjoyed such wide though brief popularity.

This attitude, however, was not apparent among the commercial publishers. Miss Foster found door after door closed in her face. As a last resort she asked the Socialistic Labor Party (SLP) in New York to publish the translation, and after some hesitation the Executive Committee entered into a contract to do so.

This was not at all to Engels' liking. "Neither Marx nor myself," he wrote to his translator early in 1886, "has ever committed the least act which might be interpreted into asking any workingmen's organization to do us any personal favor." This

---

[19] Miss Foster had been studying in Zürich for some months (FKW to MTL, June 10, 1885) and during the summer and fall of 1885 had been traveling in Europe with her mother and sister. The trip was cut short in November when Mrs. Foster suddenly died. Harper, *op. cit.,* II, 603.

stand, he explained, had been taken not only to ensure their independence, but also to forestall "bourgeois" charges of using workers' money for their own purposes.[20]

Missing the real point of Engels' caution, Florence Kelley promptly assured him in her next letter (March 1) that no personal favor had been asked in his behalf. She declared herself equally annoyed over the arrangements with the SLP—which had been made on Miss Foster's sole responsibility—"though for wholly different reasons." Her chief concern was that in the hands of the Executive Committee "the book may not have so good a start as if published by such a firm as Putnam's." The delicate problems inherent in the relationship between world leaders and local sections of a workers' movement lay as yet quite outside the range of her experience. To her the entire matter seemed an ordinary business transaction.

In general, these early letters exhibit a combination of deference and self-assurance, of quickening political zeal and exasperating (to Engels) political naiveté. Like many young people of ability, she fell into the easy assumption that competence in some fields betokens competence in any field. Widely read, and more widely experienced than the average young woman of her day, she still had only the most elementary and idealized conception of socialism both as theory and as movement.

Yet as her studies of socialist theory continued, she began to gain a deeper insight. She was in touch with affairs at home through subscriptions to a number of newspapers and magazines including the monthly *North American Review*; and her observations on the American labor and political scene, sandwiched in among the often repetitious details of translating and publishing, indicate an earnest effort to apply her new Marxist learning to an analysis and interpretation of events.

The sudden emergence in America of a national workers' movement, the Knights of Labor—which in one year had increased its membership from 104,000 to 702,000—appeared to her, as it did to Engels, a phenomenon of first rate importance. In his letter of June 3, 1886, Engels had written:

---

[20] FE to FKW, Feb. 25, 1886, p. 161. Engels first knew that Miss Foster had gone to the SLP when he read of it in the February 13 issue of *Der Sozialist,* official German language organ of the American party.

. . . the American working class is moving and no mistake. After a few false starts they will get into the right track soon enough. This appearance of the Americans upon the scene I consider one of the greatest events of the year. . . . For America after all is the ideal of all bourgeois: a country rich, vast, expanding, with purely bourgeois institutions unleavened by feudal remnants of monarchical traditions, and without a permanent and hereditary proletariat. Here everyone could become, if not a capitalist, at all events an independent man, producing and trading, with his own means, for his own account. And because there were not, *as yet,* classes with opposing interests, our—and your— bourgeois thought that America stood *above* class antago- nisms and struggles. That delusion has now broken down . . . I only wish Marx could have lived to see it! (*Engels'* *emphasis.*)

Hastening to reply, she wrote on June 9:

Your letter gave me great pleasure, the more so since it formulated what I have been thinking. . . .

The whole drama that is playing itself out before our eyes with its hundred thousands of workingmen pushed by the development of the Capitalist System to act directly in the spirit of Socialism and to make demands of our present society made by the enlightened workers of Ger- many, for instance, while the Americans are still so little enlightened that they revile and repudiate everything that bears the name of Socialism—what a commentary upon the old cry that one still hears now and then from the ideo- logues in our own ranks. "If Lasalle, Marx and Engels had not been Germans, if the Soz. Dem. agitators had never been born, there would never have been a Social Democracy in Germany!" . . .

When under the circumstances the development of the Capitalistic System forces an organization and an activity that terrifies the ruling class, the movement incarnates the Marxist theory in a way that might be instructive not only for the bourgeoisie that attributes the whole "disturbance" to "foreign Anarchists, Socialists, Communists, Nihilists and Atheists," but for some of our German leaders too, who still dream of moulding, or at least determining the pace of, the general movement.

Meanwhile, she continued, American capitalists have not been idle, but

have taken to organizing, en gros . . . and have, as I am told, formed a federation of the largest Iron, Sugar and

Textile interests for common protection. Their common fund was reported some time ago as having reached two and a half million dollars for common use, and for the especial support of small firms in resisting the demands of the organized workers. . . . The bourgeoisie shows no want of class consciousness.

On the other hand the labor movement, as she saw it, suffered from a two-fold weakness: leaders who industriously preached harmony between Capital and Labor, and workers who were

in a state of confusion incredible if it were not proved in every election. The whole presidential campaign that created so much discussion, two years ago, turned upon no principle whatsoever. The sole question was, "Who is the least of a rascal?" . . . And this morning's American mail brought, in my bourgeois daily, an announcement of a mass meeting called by the Knights of Labor in Philadelphia to demand a change in wool duties! Free Trade or Protection is the burden of the song of the politicians, and workingmen take up the chorus *now* in the midst of their own movement, so far from clear are they as to the source and meaning of the evils that beset them. And how should they be clear, with no literature, *such* political training, and a capitalist press perhaps yet more corrupt than the English?

Therefore, she repeated, the urgent need in America was for a "scientific literature" for workers.

This need, she felt, was not being met by anyone now writing in the field of American social and economic change. She had nothing but scorn for Richard T. Ely, just coming to the fore as an economist specializing in labor problems. Henry George, whose *Progress and Poverty* had appeared in 1879, she found decidedly unscientific. Even the first American popularization of Marxian economics, written by the socialist Laurence Gronlund, she dismissed as that "wretched, would-be-popular-at-all-costs *Cooperative Commonwealth.*" The long and the short of it, in her estimation, was that the immediate need could only be met by making the writings of Marx and Engels themselves directly available to the American workers.

She ended this outpouring of ideas by proposing once more,

"if no one has der Ursprung in hand," that she use the summer
to translate it, and added:

> You will be interested to know that a large section of
> the Suffrage Association in Iowa took for the subject of its
> discussions through the winter, Morgan's works, especially
> his Ancient Society.[21] The money for publishing whatever
> of yours or Marx' I may translate is in readiness at any
> time, having been placed at my disposal.

When more than a month went by without an answer she
wrote again (August 4) repeating her request, "not because I
wish to intrude, but because my free time is rapidly passing."
Engels, who had been working overtime to get the translation
of *Das Kapital* to the printer, replied a few days later, regretting
he had not known that she had "spare time for party work."
However, he had just about decided to bring out *Origin of the
Family* in England, which at the moment offered a better chance
of publishing and circulating Socialist works; and in that case
Dr. Edward Aveling had been promised the translation. Besides,
this did not seem the most appropriate work for the present
stage of American working-class development.

As an alternative, he suggested she try translating some of
the French popularizations of Marx's theories that had been
published several years earlier. "No doubt Bernstein can let
you look at a copy," he went on, ". . . and then you might judge
for yourself." Even better, he thought, would be for her to write
a series of popular pamphlets based on *Das Kapital*. "This
would be especially instructive in America, as it would give the
economic history of that country, from a land of independent
peasants to a centre of modern industry and might be completed by especially American facts."[22]

---

[21] Lewis Henry Morgan, *Ancient Society, or Researches in the Lines of Human
Progress from Savagery, through Barbarism to Civilization;* published in America
in 1877. Marx thought very highly of this work, and had made notes for a further
exposition of Morgan's conclusions, but died before he was able to begin work on it.
Engels expanded Marx's notes into *Der Ursprung der Familie, des Privateigentums
und des Staats (Origin of the Family, Private Property and the State).* "It is
Morgan's great merit," wrote Engels in his Preface to the First Edition (1884),
"that he has discovered and reconstructed in its main lines this prehistoric basis of
our written history, and that in the kinship groups of the North American Indians
he has found the key to the most important and hitherto insoluble riddles of earliest
Greek, Roman and German history."

[22] FE to FKW, Aug. 13-14, 1886, p. 160.

Barely concealing her disappointment, she nevertheless bowed to his judgment. She drew some consolation from the fact that "the Ursprung" would appear shortly, since

> I do not agree with you (*she wrote on August* 26) that for those who do read and will read there is matter enough being provided. On the contrary, I am constantly embarrassed for want of socialist literature, in English, and now when das Kapital and die Lage are made accessible, there will be need of just such other smaller scientific works as die Entwicklung, der Ursprung and others which are neither popular tracts for propaganda among the masses nor great volumes a comprehension of which requires previous training, but compact and manageable little books for young people of some general education but no specific training in the direction of economic investigation. And in America where we have scores and hundreds of little colleges all of a standard of work lower than that of the English Universities and narrow enough in the scope of work done, there is yet a mass of young people who answer to this description.

The suggestion that she herself do some writing was received with thanks if not too much enthusiasm; she was not to act on it until some time after she had returned to America.

A trip home, "for a time," had been planned since early summer (letter of June 9). She evidently expected to divide her time in the future between Europe and the United States, for she gave the Paris address of Drexel, Harjes and Company, Paris, as "my permanent address wherever I may be, whether in Zürich or New York." The visit would also serve to assure better publishing arrangements for other works. As for *Die Lage*, she wrote just before leaving (August 26), she hoped on her return to advertise it so effectively as to "force it into the book market." She and her husband, she added, would be "passing through London on our way to New York in the course of the Autumn, and I hope to have the pleasure of calling upon you."

She was indeed to have that pleasure. The Wischnewetzkys left Switzerland early in September, expecting to reach London about the middle of the month. Traveling with them was a Mme. Guillaume-Schack, formerly active in the German women's movement, now exiled and living in England, who also intended to pay her respects to Engels.[23]

Unhappily, there is no description of the visit to 122 Regent's Park Road, either in the correspondence or elsewhere. The only reference to it is in a letter from Florence Kelley to Engels after she reached New York: "It is too bad that our stay in London was so brief and our visit to you so hurried."[24]

---

[23] Friedrich Engels, Paul et Laura Lafargue, *Correspondance,* (Editions Sociales, Paris, 1959), I, 377.

Mme. Schack, born a member of the German nobility, had married and divorced a Swiss painter named Guillaume, brother of the anarchist James Guillaume. Because of the anti-Socialist laws she had made her home in England since the summer of 1885, and was well known in Liberal and radical (sometimes anarchist) circles. Engels considered her "harmless" but recommended caution in dealing with someone of such "overflowing impulsiveness." Engels, *Briefe an Bernstein,* May 5, 1887, p. 191 and note.

[24] The memoirs simply state: "The author [of *Die Lage*] I saw but once. That was in London on our way to America." *The Survey,* April 1, 1927, p. 34. Actually there was one other brief encounter, in the summer of 1888. See below, pp. 95 ff.

CHAPTER VI

The Commitment vs. The Bureaucracy

The New York that greeted the Wischnewetzkys in the fall of 1886 was a city in which bitter economic conflict had finally pushed the labor movement into the political arena. The winter before, the country as a whole had been shaken by a series of successful strikes led by the Knights of Labor. But in the spring the railroad strikes in the Southwest against Jay Gould had been smashed, and this, together with the May 4 Haymarket Riot and its aftermath of repression had brought an end to the wave of labor victories. By early summer the more politically minded of the Knights, carrying a reluctant T. V. Powderly with them, had decided that legislative and electoral action was their only recourse.[1]

In the city itself, local labor leaders were coming to the same conclusion, and for like reasons. Transit workers, on strike against a twelve- to sixteen-hour day and the miserly wage that went with it, had been met with police violence and whole-sale arrests. The same treatment was meted out to employees boycotting the Thiess Brewery. In the midst of all this, in April the Board of Aldermen almost to a man was indicted for bribe-taking.

Several months later, New York newspapers were carrying the story that the unions planned to take an active part in the November mayoralty elections. The candidate under consideration was Henry George, now celebrated as the author of *Progress and Poverty*, and recently returned from a triumphant tour of Europe. In August a committee representing some 165 labor organizations visited George and asked him to be the "workingman's candidate" for mayor on the United Labor

---

[1] Norman J. Ware, *The Labor Movement in the United States, 1860-1896* (New York & London, 1929), pp. 360-61.

Party ticket. After twice declining for fear that a small vote would do no good either to him or his cause, he was persuaded to accept when more than 34,000 pledges of support were presented to him.[2]

Up to then both Tammany Hall and the County Democracy faction had been preparing for a campaign-as-usual. The Republican candidate, an energetic young lawyer named Theodore Roosevelt, held no terrors for them. But the unexpected surge of support for George, most of it coming from normally Democratic ranks, upset all their calculations.

When George refused to be bribed out of the race—Tammany Boss Croker and the County Democracy promised him a seat in Congress if he would withdraw—the machine called upon Abram S. Hewitt to be the Democratic candidate. Hewitt, a prosperous iron manufacturer and long a leader in the reform group in Tammany Hall, was dumbfounded by such an offer coming from the "regulars." But after thinking it over in the light of events and Henry George, he decided it was his duty to run, and in his acceptance speech pledged among other things to save New York from the "ideas of anarchists, nihilists, communists, socialists, and mere theorists."[3]

This was in early October, at about the time that Florence Kelley and her husband were getting settled, finding first a temporary residence at 3 Livingston Place, and shortly after, more permanent quarters at 110 East 76th Street. She was expecting a second child within a few weeks, but with all her domestic problems she still found time to follow the campaign with keenest interest.

Her first letter to Engels from America, dated November 13 and apparently devoted only to problems of publication, never reached him.[4] But in a second letter, written December 10 sometime after the birth of her daughter Margaret, she sent him a graphic thumbnail sketch of the election activities.

> I wish from the bottom of my heart (*she wrote*) that you could have been here during the campaign. . . . At first

[2] Henry George, Jr., *The Life of Henry George* (New York, 1900), p. 459; Anna George De Mille, *Henry George, Citizen of the World* (Chapel Hill, 1950), pp. 142 ff.

[3] Allan Nevins, *Abram S. Hewitt, with some account of Peter Cooper* (New York & London, 1935), pp. 460-62; H. George, Jr., *op. cit.*, p. 473.

[4] FKW to FE, Dec. 10, 1886; FE to FKW, Dec. 28, 1886, p. 165.

110 *East 76th Street*

Closeup of doorway

Henry George

the leaders of the old parties declined to make any personal campaign, but kept in the background in lofty disdain, but after about a week, when George and the workingmen had been holding eight meetings every night, indoors and out, with thousands of voters at each, Mr. Hewitt gradually emerged from his calm retreat; and before the close of the campaign the poor, broken down, old gentleman was racing about wherever they could get a crowd together, by day and by night, in fair weather and foul, in the open street and in all sorts of halls; and that after he had declared that his health did not permit him to meet George in a debate in Chickering Hall!

Although the character of his campaign, with the impressive vote garnered, seems to have somewhat modified her earlier opinion of George, it did not alter her objections to his economic and social policies, nor change her conviction that the preface to *Die Lage* must deal critically with both the man and the movement.

The point which makes a preface so urgently needed (*she wrote in the same letter*) is the sudden importance of the George movement. You know Mr. George's limitations from his books. His idee fixe is the land, and however much quickness and Entwicklungsfähigkeit Mr. George himself may possess, his followers are sticking fast at the land question even more than himself. Here is an item that will give you a glimpse into Mr. George's present economic thinking. I gave one of his friends a copy of the Introduction to the Lage, and she showed it to him. He halted at the first sentence. "The history of the proletariat in England begins with the second half of the century, with the invention of the steam engine and of machinery for working cotton," and said: "No! That is where they are all wrong," and proceeded to expound at length and with great vigor, that since land has been held as private property there have always been proletarians—using the word as synonymous with *toiler*, in general, or *poor man*, and utterly oblivious to the specific character of the proletariat. Yet he is far in advance of most of his co-laborers; and he and they are so immensely active, and the real enlightenment among the workers is so very limited; and the literature available for meeting the present vast demand is so pitifully scanty (Gronlund, Ely!) that there is dire need of one thorough definition of our position towards Mr. George and his movement; or, perhaps I should say, a characterization of his theory.

In his reply (December 28) Engels first congratulated her "on the happy family event in which you have been the principal actor," and added best wishes for her health and that of her daughter. He then pointed out that the kind of analysis she was asking for would require more study than he was presently in a position to undertake; nor was the preface the proper vehicle for it.

Always the teacher as well as the strategist, he continued:

My preface will of course turn entirely on the immense stride made by the American workingman in the last ten months, and naturally also touch H. G. and his land scheme. But it cannot pretend to deal extensively with it. Nor do I think the time for that has come. It is far more important that the movement should spread, proceed harmoniously, take root and embrace as much as possible the whole American proletariat, than that it should start from the beginning on theoretically perfectly correct lines. . . . The great thing is to get the working class to move *as a class*; that once obtained, they will soon find the right direction, and all who resist, H. G. or Powderly, will be left out in the cold with small sects of their own. Therefore I also think the K. of L. a most important factor in the movement . . . and I consider the Germans there have made a grievous mistake when they tried, in the face of a mighty and glorious movement not of their own creation, to make of their imported and not always understood theory a kind of *alleinseligmachendes* dogma, and to keep aloof from any movement which did not accept that dogma. Our theory is not a dogma but the exposition of a process of evolution, and that process involves successive phases. . . . A million or two of workingmen's votes next November for a *bona fide* workingmen's party is worth infinitely more at present than a hundred thousand votes for a doctrinally perfect platform.

In thus counselling patience to his American friend, he was at the same time administering a rebuke to those German-Americans in the SLP who had assumed the role of self-appointed mentors to the labor movement. Such presumption, in America as elsewhere, was not new. Florence Kelley herself had commented on it while still in Zürich, and she was to become even more aware of it over the next few months.

During this time she had more than enough to keep her busy. The countless details attendant upon the translation were always with her. There had been a "slow convalescence" after the birth of her little girl. On December 4 Dr. Wischnewetzky had left on a trip to Europe, and she found herself single-handedly managing a household and caring for two small children.

Nonetheless, with the enthusiasm of the George candidacy still running high, she decided not to wait for Engels, but to attempt "a definition of our position" herself. This she did in a lengthy preface to a translation she had just completed, of a speech by the Socialist physician Dr. Johann Jakoby of Königsberg,[5] entitled "The Object of the Labor Movement," which she thought would be a useful piece of educational material. Although ostensibly an evaluation of the speech, fully half of the preface was given over to her estimate of Henry George, partly based on Engels' letters, partly the result of her own thinking.

Classifying George as a Jeffersonian and an "upright Democrat (who) has placed himself on the side of the Labor Class," she saw him destined to play an honorable role in the American labor movement provided "he follows to the end the path he has entered, as we do not doubt he will do." The kernel of her criticism was that George's proposal for nationalization of the land was "totally insufficient" in a society of capitalist production. Hence his demand must be extended to include "socialization of *all* the means of production" if he is to become "the true representative of the workers.'" But if he fails thus to place himself "upon the standpoint of modern scientific Socialism . . . he will be condemned to be a mere leader of a sect."

Turning then to Jakoby's speech, she found herself as a Socialist at odds with him on two points: his declaration that profit-sharing was desirable for and desired by workers, and his assumption that "the State and Capitalist Class" will try to solve the labor question peacefully. The first she characterized as "a trick of the employer . . . to buy peace from (his) employees"; she disagreed with the second because

> . . . the state becomes year by year more completely the property, the willing tool, of these same corporations and less capable of actions in the interests of the people . . .

---

[5] Dr. Jakoby, a leader of the left wing of the Prussian National Assembly since 1848, had delivered the speech to his constituents in 1870. Two years later he joined the German Social Democratic Party. He was highly regarded by the early German Socialists.

The transition from the Wage-System to the Socialistic
Organization of society is going on around us, and its peaceful consummation clearly rests with the Working Class.
The clearer the insight of the workers, the speedier and
more peaceful the change.

It is not without interest that she also introduced into her
preface some ideas that were later to form the heart of her work
as a social reformer—the need to prohibit employment of children under fourteen and to enforce this prohibition with adequate inspection; and the need for sufficient school accommodations bolstered by "an efficiently enforced compulsory law."

Having completed her first independent contribution, she
arranged for its printing by the New York Labor News Company, publishing arm of the SLP.[6] In the meantime the
Workmen's Advocate, English language organ of the Party, ran
the translation in five installments (January 22 to February
19, 1887), and in its February 5 issue printed her preface.

There is no doubt that at this time Florence Kelley saw herself as prepared to play a significant role in American radical
circles. She had much to recommend her—her Zürich experiences; her relationship with Engels and, on her return to this
country, a newly acquired friendship with one of Engels' closest
associates, Friedrich Sorge;[7] her active participation as a member of the New York section of the SLP; and not least, her ties
by birth and training to the American tradition. Yet these very
assets became liabilities when, through a series of incidents
that erupted in the early months of 1887, she found herself
caught up in a tangle of blunders, misunderstandings and accusations that were to place a severe strain on her relations with
Engels, and to end in the expulsion from the party of both her
husband and herself.

The circumstances that led to such a pass were for the most
part not of her making, but were grounded, although she was
never fully aware of it, in the special problems inherent in her
membership in the SLP. An American whose ancestry reached

---

[6] Johann Jakoby, *The Object of the Labor Movement*, Preface by Florence Kelley-
Wischnewetzky, translated by Florence Kelley-Wischnewetzky (New York Labor
News Co., 1887). The pamphlet was reprinted by the same company in 1892.

[7] Friedrich A. Sorge (1827-1906), former secretary of the First International, was
now living in Hoboken, N. J., with his wife.

back to colonial times, she had pushed her way into what was essentially a private world of German-American socialists. The inhabitants of that world knew nothing about her; and she knew next to nothing of their past history, continuing sensitivities and present doctrinal preoccupations. Speaking almost no English, isolated, ingrown, and all the more jealous of autonomy, they keenly resented any hint of criticism or interference, even —perhaps especially—from the world leader of their movement. And while Florence Kelley was never that emissary the SLP officials may have imagined her to be, her impetuous nature and her proprietary attitude toward Engels did very little to dispel such a notion.

The SLP had been founded some ten years earlier through a merger of three independent Socialist groups. From its inception it had been plagued by a running internal battle between the Marxists who stood for building socialist strength within the trade unions, and the followers of Ferdinand Lasalle who pressed for independent socialist political action. After 1879 another source of friction appeared—the anarchist doctrines brought in by some of the refugees from Bismarck's anti-Socialist laws.

By 1883 the party had sunk to its lowest figure, 1500 members in no more than thirty sections. Only sixteen delegates registered at its national convention that year. But 1883 also marked the beginning of a national depression that revived interest in socialism as a solution to economic distress. In the next two years (1884-1886) the SLP tripled its membership. An official German language weekly, *Der Sozialist,* was founded, and the New Haven *Workmen's Advocate* was taken over as the official English language daily. In the fall of 1886 the SLP was able to play a significant role in the birth of the United Labor Party and in the George campaign as well.[8]

For a time, the wave of invigorating electoral activity tended to submerge the party's usual dogmatic treatment of policy and people. But as the campaign receded the old narrow attitudes and bureaucratic practices again asserted themselves.

---

[8] Howard H. Quint, *The Forging of American Socialism* (University of South Carolina Press, 1953), pp. 13, 16, 23-25. SLP leaders were accredited delegates at the organizational meetings of the United Labor Party (p. 38).

Engels, watching from across the ocean, understood quite well that the George campaign had not rid the SLP of sectarian ways. He could not of course intervene directly; but the preface to *Die Lage* would provide an opportunity for a broadly constructive albeit critical evaluation of the party. This evaluation he had summarized in his December letter to Florence Kelley.

A full account of her part in the complex of events that followed is hampered by some gaps in the correspondence. Three of her letters are missing—those of January 28, March 19 "postmarked April 8th," and April 18—and one of Engels' dated April 27. But we do have a long letter written by Engels February 9, and three of hers dated April 25, April 26 and May 2; and these enable us to reconstruct much of what occurred during the winter and spring months of 1887.

Her difficulties appear to have fallen into two main categories, those clustered about the printing of *Die Lage,* and the ones relating to the "Aveling affair"; although there were others, too, minor but irritating.

One such dates from early in January. She seems to have discussed Engels' December letter with someone in the SLP leadership. For shortly afterwards the *Workmen's Advocate* printed a paragraph in which the point Engels had made about the value of a large vote for a *"bona fide* workingmen's party" was twisted into

> . . . it is of more importance that the workingmen should cast one million of votes at the first national election in which they participate, even though such votes be cast at random and without definite object, than that 100,000 votes should be cast for definite objects and principles.

In an indignant reply headed "A Defense of Engels,"[9] Florence Kelley berated the paper for having "put in Engels' mouth such a piece of nonsense" and for labelling it his "expressed opinion." She herself, she continued, was indeed privy to Engels' opinion, but would never think of publishing it without permission. There was no public follow-up to this exchange, but Engels, receiving an account of it from her a few days later, was more than vexed.

The first frictions over *Die Lage* had developed while she was

---

[9] *Workmen's Advocate,* Jan. 29, 1887, 4:2.

still in Zürich. After the manuscript was accepted, there had been a long delay until she received proof. "I am disturbed at the quality of paper, type and workmanship," she had written Engels (May 31, 1886), "and have written Miss Foster . . . urging her to insist upon having the book published in a form proportional to the high price which she paid for it."

Once arrived in New York, she could and did take over supervision of the proceedings, but apparently was not able to hasten them appreciably. "Anyone at a distance," she wrote Engels, "unable to follow all the details (as our good friend Herr Sorge has done) could never imagine all the ramifications of the process of delay and annoyance." These ramifications were not made explicit at the time, but finances were a large part of them. "Miss Foster paid the S.A.P. [Sozialistische Arbeiter-Partei] Exec. Com. $500. to issue the book and they had squandered the money," Florence Kelley was to write later. There was continuing dissatisfaction on her part with the workmanship, while the other side complained that her demands for changes and corrections were driving up production costs.

But these were petty annoyances beside the sequence of events that came to be known as the "Aveling affair."

In the fall of 1886 Edward Aveling, with Karl Marx's daughter Eleanor Marx-Aveling and the veteran German Socialist Wilhelm Liebknecht, had come to the United States for an extended lecture tour under the auspices of the SLP. The tour began in Hartford, Connecticut, on September 14, continued through New York State and the principal cities of New Jersey and Pennsylvania, then moved west to Chicago and Detroit and as far as Minnesota, south to Kansas City and Louisville, through Ohio, to Baltimore and back to New York City, covering some fifty cities in all. Most of the audiences were large and enthusiastic; but even where the "Red scare" of the previous spring still lingered it was possible to bring together small gatherings.[10]

The National Executive Committee expressed great satisfaction with the results of the tour—until the time came for a

---

[10] An account of this tour was published as *The Working Class Movement in America*, by Edward Aveling and Eleanor Marx-Aveling, Swan Sonnenschein, Lowrey & Co., London, 1888.

financial settlement. Aveling had presented weekly expense
accounts which apparently were received without question. But
at an NEC meeting on December 23, two days before he and
Eleanor were to return to England, some objections were raised
to the figures presented for a final accounting. According to
presently available correspondence (Engels to Sorge, Engels to
Florence Kelley-Wischnewetzky), Dr. Aveling declared he
would not "bargain" with the party but would be satisfied with
whatever settlement the NEC chose to make.

During the course of the meeting an issue was introduced
that had been the subject of considerable and heated debate for
some months—the attitude of the SLP toward the Knights of
Labor. Against strong opposition by some of the NEC members,
Aveling had repeatedly urged the closest cooperation between
the party and the Knights. At a mass meeting the day before
he had said: "The best Knights of Labor come from the Socialists, and the best Socialists make the best Knights of Labor."[11]
In the committee meeting he seems to have been sharper and
more specific. It would be stupid and egotistical, he said, to
hold aloof from the Knights of Labor, since, by joining, it would
be possible to win over the members, or at least a part of them,
for socialism. As the *Volkszeitung* reported it (December 24),
the meeting ended soon after in a friendly spirit, and with hearty
thanks from Aveling for the support and cooperation given
him on his tour.

A week later, however (December 30), a highly sensational-
ized report of the meeting appeared in the *New York Herald*.
According to this story, the Committee had honored Aveling's
weekly expense accounts, but had balked at a supplementary
bill for such items as corsages for Mrs. Aveling, theatre tickets,
wine, "cigars (for) the doctor and cigarettes (for) his emanci-
pated lady." After "many harsh words" one of the Committee
members was said to have flung $100 at the Avelings, saying,
"Here is enough to pay your passage back to England. We are
glad to get rid of you." Dr. Aveling "looked thoroughly mad,"
the *Herald* continued, but took the money; and just before
sailing lodged a protest with the NEC against the "brutal treat-

---

[11] *New Yorker Volkszeitung*, Dec. 22, 1886. The *Volkszeitung*, a socialist daily,
was founded in 1878. The editors were Dr. Adolph Douai and Alexander Jonas.

ment" accorded him and his wife because of the expense accounts. The *Herald* made no mention of the policy disagreement over the Knights of Labor. It centered its attention on the financial dispute, and poured out almost a column of disparaging comment in a patent effort to discredit the entire socialist movement.

As the December 23 meeting had taken place behind closed doors, any information in the *Herald* beyond what had appeared in the *Volkszeitung* presumably had been "leaked." Evidently, dissension within the SLP had become so serious that one faction would deliberately turn to a "capitalist" medium in an effort to discredit the other.

The *New York Daily Tribune* picked up the story, and on the following day printed its own version, less sensational but scarcely more flattering. It noted that on the money question "Everybody appeared to be satisfied and they shook hands all round." With regard to the "interesting little quarrel" over the Knights of Labor, which the paper headlined as a factional split, the *Tribune* quoted as Dr. Aveling's parting shot: "Any Socialist who does not join the Knights of Labor is an egotistical idiot." The *Tribune* account included an interview with SLP Secretary William Rosenberg, who in the course of it acknowledged that "perhaps we were a little short with them." He added that both the protest, which he called presumptuous, "and the question as to whether we shall have to censure Dr. Aveling, will have to be decided by the committee at its next meeting."

The situation was further inflamed when the *Herald* story was reprinted in the London *Times*,[12] thus giving it international currency. When the Avelings saw the article, they immediately issued a "circular" of protest which they sent not only to the NEC but to all the American sections and to party leaders in the Old World as well. Neither they nor Engels knew at the time that the NEC had already circularized the sections with a communication so worded as to make Aveling appear a veritable swindler.[13]

---

[12] FE to F. Sorge, March 16, 1887. *Letters to Americans,* pp. 179-80. All of Engels' letters to Sorge here cited are from this source.

[13] FE to FKW, Feb. 9, 1887, p. 172. Of the NEC Engels wrote to Sorge (Mar. 16, 1887, p. 179): "But the meanest of all is that it sent out its circular over there on

Florence Kelley, as we know from Engels' reply, sent him a lengthy letter on January 28, in which she enclosed the *Workmen's Advocate* distortion of Engels' views and her answer, and also wrote a full account of the Aveling incident. She had apparently accepted the NEC version as put forth in their circular, and had approved a subsequent resolution of the New York sections to alert the European parties. She even went so far as to recommend "giving Kautsky a hint, not to let any [material] appear which [is] advertised in the name of Aveling," since "his name . . . can only injure any organ."[14]

Engels' reaction was immediate and angry. He first took her sharply to task for having shown his December letter to anyone. "The passage about the hundred thousand and millions," he wrote, "occurred in my letter to you and in *no other letter.* So you will know who is responsible . . . for putting this nonsense into my mouth."

But his greater wrath was turned on her for having judged Aveling guilty after hearing only one side of the story. What really infuriated the old man was that the accusation implied complicity on the part of Eleanor Marx,

> and then it becomes utterly absurd, in my eyes at least. Her I have known from a child, and for the past seventeen years she has been constantly about me. And more than that, I have inherited from Marx the obligation to stand by his children as he would have done himself, and to see, as far as lies in my power, that they are not wronged. And that I shall do, in spite of fifty Executives. The daughter of Marx swindling the working class—too rich indeed![15]

January 7th, but sent it to us only on *February 3rd,* so that it gained a whole month's unhampered headstart in its calumnies before we even learned what A[veling] was really accused of."

[14] FE to FKW, Feb. 9, 1887, p. 173. Engels quotes these remarks of hers back to her. The specific "organ" meant was *Die Neue Zeit,* of which Kautsky was one of the editors.

[15] *Ibid.,* p. 171. Although Aveling may have been unjustly accused in this instance, his character generally left much to be desired. That he worked assiduously and effectively for many years in the Socialist movement is indispuntable. But he was always lax in financial matters, borrowing indiscriminately and neglecting to repay. He never hesitated to use his charm on any woman who caught his fancy, even while living in common-law union with Eleanor Marx. When his legal wife, from whom he had long been separated, finally died (1898), he secretly married a young actress, and Eleanor, broken-hearted, committed suicide. Engels, who died in 1895, apparently never saw Aveling's faults and constantly defended him. Bernstein writes that "many people kept away from Engels' house" whenever Aveling was there; and he was *persona non grata* elsewhere as well. Cf. Bernstein, *op. cit.,* pp. 161-63, 202-3; and

Such a vehement rejoinder put the matter in a different light, and the Wischnewetzkys began to ask some questions of their own. They soon became convinced that an injustice had been done and did not hesitate to say so, although of this Engels was not immediately made aware.

In the meantime his preface to *Die Lage* had arrived, and what had been merely technical disputes over publication of the book suddenly became political ones. He had written a section on the SLP that was a balanced appraisal of the deficiencies as well as the strengths of the party. The leaders, however, saw only the criticism, which they considered unfounded. To make matters worse, the Wischnewetzkys decided, without party consultation, to publish the preface in English and German as a pamphlet for mass distribution. At this point work on *Die Lage,* already slowed by innumerable delays, came to a dead stop; whereupon the contract was terminated and the unbound sheets turned over to the publishing firm of John W. Lovell and Company to complete. On April 26 Florence Kelley wrote with relief: "The book is out."

The reversal of their stand on Aveling, and their questioning of Executive Commiteee motives, had another consequence for the Wischnewetzkys. On April 1 the NEC brought charges against them for "making an unjustified accusation."[16] Shortly thereafter the two were suspended by the local body when Dr. Wischnewetzky called the Executive a "trauriges unter-suchungs com[mittee]" and was overheard by a Central Committeeman. "I was at home with the babies when the atrocity was said to have been committed!" Florence Kelley wrote on April 26. As a result, she continued,

> We've been suspended for a few days for Majestäts belei-digung and when the preface gets well into circulation we shall probably be suspended again for Verbreitung ver-botener Schriften. The Executive does not like the preface and is burying it in impenetrable silence. The Sozialist never mentions the book except for purposes of misrepresentation and has suppressed my reply to the last dose for

Havelock Ellis, "Eleanor Marx," in *Modern Monthly* (September, 1935), pp. 285, 289-90, 295.

[16] "In folge einer von Gen. Wischnewetski gegen die National-Exekutive erhoben ungerechtfertigen Beschuldigung wird beschlossen Anklage zu erheben." N. E. K. Sitzung, 1 April. In *Der Sozialist,* April 23, 1887.

three weeks past. The Volkszeitung is open to us; but we did not want to rush into print without trying to settle matters in the regular order of appeal.

So absorbed in the battles over *Die Lage* and Aveling, she probably did not realize that Engels' February letter had actually gone unanswered. She had not written again until March 19, and then only to ask permission to reprint the Preface in German. Her letter of April 18 merely mentioned that she had "nothing to report" about Aveling.

To Engels this must have appeared downright evasion; from her remark about Kautsky he may have suspected that she had done some meddling on the international scene. At any rate, it is clear that he directed a second, harsher blast at her in the missing letter of April 27, and had even been on the point of making its contents public.

Shaken by such a turn, she dashed off an agitated reply (May 2) by the next mail. Eleven pages long and not entirely legible, the letter expressed both self-reproach and self-justification, and at the same time denounced the SLP leaders for double dealing.

> Dear Mr. Engels (*she wrote*), Your letter of Apr. 27th is at hand. In reply, I would say that, in the matter of publishing letters, your printing yours would have involved my printing mine, because I hold your construction of much that was in mine erroneous. But that is a subordinate matter, and I was glad the case did not arise. I only mention it because I regret most keenly having written that letter and earnestly hope it may not be further magnified. I heartily wish to make an end of the subject, the more so as we were perfectly passive in regard to it, except in so far as writing that letter to you and speaking to our common friend Sorge. . . .
>
> I must honestly say that I do not feel remorseful in not having assumed in advance that the Executive was one nine-fold rascal. . . .
>
> What I do regret, and that lesson I have learned for the rest of my life, is that I did, like the whole body of members, found my *opinion* upon the presentation of one side of the matter. And yet, (except that letter to you) in our *action* we did instinctively await the hearing of both sides. Then, having both sides, we protested most vigorously against the Executive's betrayal and deceit. . . .

Nor had I any reason to suppose at the time that Rosenberg told a deliberate lie when he assured Dr. Wischnewetzky and me, that a detailed letter to you from himself had been sent before the second meeting was held in the matter, and that the circular was forwarded to you immediately upon its publication. . . .

My mention of Mr. Kautsky was simply because he was your friend, at work near you, to whom you could speak. . . . I never so much as wrote to personal friends in Zürich about it.

I thought of your having no direct unofficial report, and reported things here at the time; and when I wrote you April 18th that I had nothing to report it was because several points in Dr. Aveling's defense and circular left the matter between him and the Executive far from clear in my mind; so that, as between the two, I saw no reason to change my first opinion, however, much I might distrust and despise the Executive.

The issues became clear, she continued, only after a second circular by the Executive appeared, and she "immediately acted accordingly." That action was to make two demands:

first, Revocation of the resolutions voted in the Aveling matter on the ground that they all rested upon deception and fraud, because if the two lines of Dr. Aveling's letter of Dec. 18th to the Executive, in which he says he makes no objection to anything which the Treasurer may strike, had been laid before the Party in the first place, no such resolutions would have been voted; and second, das Herauspeitschen desjenigen mitgliedes aus der Partei welches die Geschichte an der Herald verkauft hat, desto mehr die Geruchte immer mehr laut werden dass dasselbe in der Exekutive sitzt. . . .[17]

I think you will see from our whole action that there is no necessity for further controversial correspondence, and I am sure I desire it as little as yourself.

Having delivered herself of the full story, she then turned briefly to other matters. She observed that "your preface proves more and more a propos"; noted that Henry George seemed "indeed in the act of settling down into the leader of a sect"; and concluded with the hope "that your eye is growing well."

---

[17] "the expulsion from the Party of that member who sold the story to the Herald, all the more since the rumor continues to spread that that same person sits in the Executive."

During the height of the Aveling controversy, throughout February, March and April, Engels had channelled his discussion of tactics, as well as his irritation, through Friedrich Sorge. The latter in turn was receiving the troubled confidences of Florence Kelley as she began to understand the situation more fully. Sorge seems to have acted as an escape valve for Engels, whose letters at this point bristled with ill-humored characterizations of his hapless translator: "a weak person, influenced by every gust of wind"; "she translates like a factory"; "she has neglected (the) publishing miserably"; "Mrs. Wischnewetzky has bungled everything she has handled." Sorge, having the other side of the story, finally calmed him down with a letter (April 26) in which he conveyed the Wischnewetzkys' sincere regrets for the part they had unintentionally played in the Aveling matter. Thus mollified, Engels, without waiting for Florence Kelley's reply to his letter of April 27, sent her a forgiving message (May 7) and declared that as far as he was concerned the incident was closed.[18]

What stands out most clearly in this period is Florence Kelley's effort to keep her balance in the midst of a difficult and bewildering situation. On the one hand she found herself in inevitable collision with the bureaucratic rigidities of the SLP, embroiled as it was in a factionalism that seemed to make very little sense in view of the genuine issues of the day. On the other hand, she had been assailed by Engels for doing what at the time she thought was her clear and only duty.

Although particularly unhappy at incurring Engels' displeasure, she was not afraid to stand up to him when she felt justified in so doing. Her suspension, and that of her husband, she could take in stride as a hazard of an immature movement disfigured by crippling sectarianism. Of the basic soundness of the principles of that movement she had not the slightest doubt. And from this experience she may have drawn still another lesson —that even the best of theories do not automatically bestow their excellence upon those who espouse them.

---

[18] FE to F. Sorge, pp. 182-86, *passim.* Sorge's April 26 letter to Engels is referred to in FE to F. Sorge, May 7, 1887, p. 186.

Friedrich A. Sorge   *Eleanor Marx-Aveling*

CHAPTER VII

"The Writer's Work of Education"

Cut off for the time being from formal contact with the SLP, Florence Kelley was all the more anxious to get on with "the writer's work of education."[1] Her translation of *Die Lage* was now well into circulation. The Jakoby pamphlet with her own preface had been launched by the *Workmen's Advocate*. Twenty thousand copies of Engels' Preface to *Die Lage* were being run off by the printing firm of Louis Weiss. A German version was to follow as soon as Engels, who was suffering from a recurrent inflammation of the eyes, could translate his English original.[2]

Her next project was of quite a different character. She had not forgotten Engels' suggestion, from her Zürich days, that she write a series of popular pamphlets based on the contents of *Capital*. She therefore sat down to compose what may have been intended as the first of such a series.

Entitled "The Need of Theoretical Preparation for Philanthropic Work," the essay was essentially an elementary lesson in Marxism. Before handing it over to be printed, she read it at the May meeting of the New York chapter of the Association

---

[1] This was a phrase she had used in her letter on the George campaign, in describing the aftermath: "All eyes are turned towards the writer's work of education; newspapers are being founded or enlarged, and the demand for literature and lectures cannot be met." FKW to FE, Dec. 10, 1886.

[2] Alexander Jonas, editor of the *Volkszeitung*, had printed his own German translation some weeks earlier in that paper, and had offered to turn over the plates to the Wischnewetzkys (FKW to FE, April 26, 1887). Engels would have nothing to do with such "a thoroughly dull translation, containing errors to boot" (FE to F. Sorge, May 7, 1887) and declared he would write his own.

Distribution of the Preface in English, titled *The Labor Movement in America*, began in May. By mid-June the German version appeared as *Die Arbeiterbewegung in Amerika*, Vorwort zur englischen Ausgabe der "Lage der arbeitenden Klasse in England in 1844" von Friedrich Engels. Separat-Abdruck. Herausgegeben von Florence Kelley-Wischnewetzky und Dr. L. Wischnewetzky, New York, 64 und 66 Ann Str. Ecke William, 1887.

of Collegiate Alumnae.[3] As she wrote Engels later, enclosing a reprint:

> ... Their National Assn. is scattered all over the Union and numbers nearly a thousand members. This little pamphlet (accompanied by yours in German and English) will thus be brought into nearly every university in the country. .... The real excuse for writing it, when the pressure of work made it impossible to work it out with necessary thoroughness was this, that the Alumnae promised to publish it in several thousand copies and it gave the opportunity of recommending the literature of the subject.[4]

It is interesting that she chose this topic for this audience at this time. She may have felt that while Engels was speaking eloquently to American workers, no one so far had attempted to discuss socialism with any part of the American middle class in terms of their daily life and activity. These were college graduates seated in front of her, many of whom planned to carry on their life's work in the field of social service and reform. How much more effective they would be if they labored in the light of socialist understanding!

In the letter to Engels she referred to her paper as "a hurried work written in the intervals of daily drudgery," but the lack of orderly structure is only a minor drawback. Writing with emotion as well as vigor, she undertook to analyze the institution of philanthropy from the viewpoint of a Socialist.[5] Her aim was to inquire into both the philosophy and the efficacy of long-standing practices which, feeble at best, were now totally inadequate in face of the accelerating industrial process.

She began by examining the conditions that made philanthropy necessary. Society, she told her hearers, is divided into

[3] In: Backus [Mrs. Helen Hiscock] *The Need and Opportunity for College Trained Women in Philanthropic Work* (New York, 1887). The meeting took place on May 14. It is mentioned in Marion Talbot and Lois K. M. Rosenberry, *History of the American Association of University Women, 1881-1951* (Boston and New York, 1931), p. 237.

[4] FKW to FE, Aug. 28, 1887. "Your paper on philanthropy has not yet come to hand," Engels replied (FE to FKW, Sept. 15, 1887, p. 191); there is no further comment on it.

[5] This was not the first time she had questioned the validity of the methods of social assistance. Two years earlier she had written Mary Lewis (June 10, 1885): "... you can make your own work more effective if you first see clearly its complex relations. Without the broader insight, which can't be had without study and criticism, this same work may prove in the end what most philanthropic work already is, vain struggle to patch and palliate an evil social system, so propping up what ought to be torn down and rebuilt."

two diametrically opposed classes, "the smaller class owning all the necessaries of life, all the means of production . . . the larger class . . . owning nothing but (its) labor power." This division produces two kinds of philanthropy, bourgeois and working class—a differentiation of special importance to her audience.

Bourgeois philanthropy, she explained, is one of palliatives and of restitution. The capitalist system, by robbing the workers of most of the values they produce, creates poverty, disease and crime. Charitable and similar institutions attempt some alleviation after the damage is done, but they do not and cannot affect the conditions that make their work necessary. The capitalists pay back, in contributions to these charities, a very small part of what they take away through exploitation. By the partial relief thus afforded, they hope to control the "dependent and dangerous classes," and so preserve the system.

Working class philanthropy, on the other hand, is *reciprocal* and *mutual*. Through their trade unions and sick benefit societies, workers help and strengthen each other. By such demands as a shorter working day and a limitation on child labor, they "aim heavy blows at the production of surplus value, and conserve their strength for the eventual struggle to abolish the system under which they, and with them the whole of society, suffer."

Because, as she reminded her audience, most college graduates belong by birth and education to the class that not only practices bourgeois philanthropy but is responsible for the conditions that make it necessary, the question "we graduates" must answer is: ". . . where do I belong?" And she goes on:

> Shall I cast my lot with the oppressors, content to patch and darn, to piece and cobble at the worn and rotten fabric of a perishing society? Shall I spend my life in applying palliatives, in trying to make the intolerable endurable yet a little longer? . . . Shall I send a score or a hundred children for recreation to the country, while year by year our factories and tenement house work rooms demand fresh thousands of children to toil within their noisome prison walls? . . . Shall I fritter away the days of my youth investigating the deservingness of this or that applicant for relief when the steady march of industrial development throws a million able-bodied workers out of employ-

ment . . . ? Shall I not make common cause with these, my brothers and my sisters, to make an end of such a system?

In thus challenging her listeners she also made explicit the dilemma an honest answer would entail. To end the sufferings of the working class one must indeed put an end to exploitation; "but to stop exploiting would be suicide for the class that we are born and educated into, and of which we college bred women form an integral part."

Perhaps aware of the anguished—and angry—response such reasoning would evoke, she tried to anticipate some likely objections. There was no question, she emphasized, as to the "honorable and noble intention that animates" those who practice philanthropy. There was, however, a very serious question as to the effectiveness of all their work. More than that, she contended, not only were the women sitting before her in no position to evaluate results, they were not even conscious of their inability to do so. College graduates they might be, but the very colleges they attended were class institutions, "manned by . . . carefully selected employees," whose teachings were a "dogmatic apology for society as it is." As a result, the graduates of such institutions were totally devoid of the theoretical preparation that would lead to an understanding of the social system. Such preparation must therefore be found elsewhere, through a course of self-study.

To this end she offered a list of readings. As preliminary studies she proposed Laurence Gronlund's *The Cooperative Commonwealth*[6] and August Bebel's *Women in the Past, Present and Future.* The next step should be a study of Lewis Morgan's *Ancient Society,* and the "brilliant popularization, elaboration and condensation of this work," *The Origin of the Family* by Engels. By then the student would be ready for *The Condition of the Working Class in England* (she cited it without mentioning herself as translator); and, finally, for "the fundamental work *par excellence* [in] modern scientific political economy," Karl Marx's *Capital,* which "has, within the past half year been made accessible to English readers."

With this course of study, she assured her listeners, they would acquire a view of society that would enable them to com-

---

[6] Evidently she had changed her opinion of that "wretched popularization."

prehend the dynamics of the class struggle and to recognize that "the future rests with the workers." And on the basis of this altered view, the role of philanthropy and of the college graduate would then take on a completely new dedication and purpose:

> To cast our lot with the workers, to seek to understand the laws of social and industrial development . . . to spread this enlightenment among the men and women destined to contribute to the change to a higher social order, to hasten the day when all the good things of society shall be the goods of all the children of men, and our petty philanthropy of today superfluous—this is the true work for the elevation of the race, this is the true philanthropy.

There are no extant minutes of the discussion that followed this unorthodox treatment of a familiar subject, and so we have no record of how the paper was received. Nor do we know of any comment by other Association members to whom the printed essay was mailed.

Quite a storm was provoked, however, when early in June the weekly *Christian Union* ran the essay in two slightly abridged installments.[7]

> The editors received over eighty letters of inquiry and remonstrance (*Florence Kelley wrote Engels August* 28), and I was showered with books, pamphlets and letters from all parts of the country, while the Christian Union printed three editorial protests and two several-columns long protests from readers.

Of the latter, one was a signed article by Vida D. Scudder,[8] decrying "intense radicals who foster class hatred" and taking issue with the "bitter tone" of the essay as "the product of a very different social and industrial climate from our own." Miss Scudder admitted the harsh conditions afflicting so many—"the law of the survival of the fittest is inexorable." But she could offer only "the idea and ideal of brotherhood . . . [as] the ameliorative force" for the relief of distress which, through "the selfish inertia . . . of the capitalist class," was too often ignored.

---

[7] June 2 and June 9, 1887. Lyman Abbott was editor-in-chief at the time. In 1893 the *Christian Union's* name was change to *The Outlook*.

[8] Miss Scudder was later to be associated with the founding of College Settlement, at 95 Rivington Street, in New York. For her long-time interest in Christian Socialism, see her *Socialism and Character* (Boston and New York, 1912).

The other "protest," an unsigned communication from "A Worker," fastened upon Florence Kelley's married name and went on to attribute her foreign ideas to her foreign background.

Without mentioning Miss Scudder by name, Florence Kelley replied[9] both to her and to the anonymous writer, sharply rebuking those critics who "occupy themselves more with my imputed nationality and my attitude of mind than with the subject, the economic basis of the whole discussion being lost to sight." Nationality—("Have we not had enough of Know-nothingism?")—had nothing at all to do with the facts she cited. Her opponents, she contended, had been able only to protest, not refute, the substance of her essay. But since they considered her so biased, she added, let them read "one little book by an American Christian not a Socialist" — Henry George's *Progress and Poverty*. There they would find "elaborate proof" of the same charges against the American economic system that she had made.

The Philanthropy paper is the one instance we have of a full length exposition by Florence Kelley of Marxian Socialism.[10] If she had plans to follow it up with any further specific application of Marxist analysis to the American scene, those plans did not materialize. Two years elapsed before her next piece of original writing appeared, and by that time her chief concern was less with theory than with practical activity leading to social reform.

Meanwhile her great effort was to promote circulation of *Die Lage,* as well as the separately printed Preface which would serve to advertise the book. The Lovell agency seems to have distributed it fairly widely. There were reviews in the "provincial press" as well as in the newspapers of the larger cities, with the capitalist press as a whole apparently regarding the work as "one of the most dangerous publications of recent

---

[9] "A Reply," *Christian Union,* June 23, 1887, p. 27. She also took the editors to task for "mutilating" her text by some omissions.

[10] Publication of her essay by a non-socialist organ is interesting but not unusual for the time. Some months earlier (October-November, 1886), the *New York Herald* had invited its readers to write their answers to the question "What is Socialism?" and for several weeks the replies had come "flooding in" and were printed under the heading "The Pros and Cons of Socialism."

years." A collection of these reviews was sent on to Engels, who declared himself "greatly amused" by them.[11]

The socialist papers, on the other hand, received the book in silence. Except for *The Leader,* which had recently passed into socialist hands after its founding by the Central Labor Union, there was neither editorial comment nor literary review. Such few announcements as were carried consisted of paid advertisements, the money for these having come from Rachel Foster through Lovell.[12]

The same "Todtschweigen" policy was applied to the Preface. Engels had insisted on adding a footnote to the German version, specifically aimed at the SLP Executive Committee. In it he called attention to a series of articles by the Avelings which had appeared that spring in the London monthly *Time.* "I cite these excellent articles the more willingly," he wrote, "since they give me the opportunity to repudiate the miserable slanders about Aveling which the Executive of the American Socialist Labor Party has shamelessly spread abroad." (My translation.)

Even Florence Kelley felt that this was going too far, and wrote Engels asking him to delete at least the direct slap at the Executive Committee; she doubted if anyone would sell the pamphlet as it stood, or if a publisher could be found who would print it. Despite her fears, the latter problem was solved when Louis Weiss accepted the contract to print 20,000 copies of the German version. The problem of distribution she solved herself in characteristic fashion.

Although the Preface had been published separately on the sole responsibility of the Wischnewetzkys and not under party auspices, Florence Kelley had no hesitation in using the party apparatus to promote circulation. To the clubs and agents she wrote "one hundred thirty postal cards calling attention" to the pamphlets; and in response the agents ordered copies "by the hundreds."

Nor was this her only outlet. At a penny apiece or fifty cents a hundred, she wrote Engels, newsboys were glad to take batches to sell "in all the great political meetings." She had mailed sample copies to "every American organization of workingmen

---

11 FKW to FE, June 6, 1887; FE to FKW, July 20, 1887, p. 189.
12 FKW to FE, June 16, 1887.

of which I could find the address in any organ, and . . . wherever anyone holds a meeting anywhere, for propaganda I send specimens or write." Toward the end of July she spent a day making the rounds of New York newspaper offices with advance sheets of the pamphlet, urging managing editors to quote from them. Seven hundred copies went to the "National Collegiate Alumnae Association, and have borne fruit in orders for the book." Even the SLP's Labor News Company placed an order for eight hundred copies, a number of them in German. In a later report to Engels she noted that P. J. McGuire, "editor of the *Carpenter* and General Sec'y of the Brotherhood of Carpenters," (and at one time a member of the SLP,) had "taken in hand" both book and pamphlet.

In England and on the Continent the book began to make slow but noticeable progress after a somewhat shaky start. Lovell had sent an initial consignment of fifty copies to his London agent, the "Bismarckian" firm of Trübner and Company, which deliberately sabotaged distribution. After Engels transferred the agency to William Reeves, there was a gratifying increase in sales.[13] *Commonweal,* organ of the British Socialist League and edited by William Morris, (to whom Engels had personally sent a copy), ran a series of excerpts. Kautsky's *Die Neue Zeit* printed a long critical review,[14] which noted that ". . . the accurate translation by Frau Kelley-Wischnewetzky enables us to recommend the English edition to every one familiar with English and to whom the German original is not accessible." (My translation.) As for the Preface, a substantial number of copies of the English version had been put to good use in London's East End, where Dr. Aveling was lecturing on the American labor movement.[15]

Throughout the spring and summer of 1887 the Wischnewetzkys were still under the ban of suspension, and subject to mounting pressures from the Executive. But they had no inten-

---

[13] The episode involving Trübner & Co. is related in FE to FKW, Sept. 15, 1887, pp. 190-91. Reeves was publisher of much of London's popular Socialist literature, as well as the periodical *Today*. In FE to FKW, unpublished section of letter dated Dec. 3, 1887 (Sorge Collection, MSS Div., New York Public Library), Engels mentions, without seeming disturbed by it, that Reeves had "pirated" the English version of the Preface.

[14] Vol. V, pp. 529-35.

[15] FE to FKW, unpublished portion of letter of Dec. 3, 1887.

tion of letting themselves be pushed into changing their opinions, nor would they halt what they considered a good and necessary work. They had ranged themselves on the side of Engels and the Avelings, and there they stayed. They had carried through the printing and sale of the disputed Preface in spite of the certain reaction of the NEC. At the same time they were coming to regard the entire leadership as a narrow-minded clique determined to stifle all democratic procedures. As the summer wore on, the charges and countercharges became more and more violent.

Such a situation could not last, and it did not. In August the New York Section of the SLP expelled the Wischnewetzkys for "fortgesetzte Verleumdung des N. E. K."[16] As Florence Kelley described the circumstances in her letter of August 28:

> . . . the history of our expulsion is one of the most edifying chapters of the whole. There were two meetings held in the matter. At first the Investigating Committee and Rosenberg overran the meeting *at midnight* with a foolscap page full of false accusations, so that the meeting could not take any action. . . . At the second meeting a false Tagesordnung was published days in advance from which our expulsion was omitted. We therefore did not know that it was to be acted upon, were absent and were expelled in our absence.

Judging by the letters, such arbitrary action seems to have been the less disturbing to Florence Kelley since she considered it quite characteristic of the "pitiful untrustworthy mediocrities" who controlled the NEC and the New York section. In her opinion, these people in no sense represented either the party or the spirit of socialism. She was hoping to see a new leadership, worthy of the organization, elected at the national Party Congress to be held in September; and she urged Engels to express his own views in time for them to carry weight with the delegates: "The Sozialist will not close its columns to you as it does to us."

To this proposal Engels replied promptly. Having already "openly taken sides against the Executive in this matter," he wrote, he could see no value in pursuing it further. He had read of the expulsion; it was what he expected. "I am curious what

---

16 *Der Sozialist*, Aug. 27, 1887. In English, "incessant slander of the NEC."

the Congress will do," he added, "but do not hope for too much."[17]

The expulsion put no more of a damper on her activity than did the suspension. The only respite had come during the month of August and the first two weeks of September, which were spent in Gloucester, Massachusetts. Both children had been quite ill, and she had taken them north to escape the "frightful heat" of the city.

At the same time she continued to pay close attention to the shifting political scene. What especially interested her was the change in position of Henry George since the previous November. In spite of the heavy electoral support he had drawn from labor and from the socialist movement, by mid-summer he had broken with both. The program he had advanced for the coming United Labor Party convention completely ignored all the labor planks that had strengthened his mayoralty campaign; and on August 5, ULP secretary McMackin ruled that the party would no longer welcome members of the SLP.[18] The next day George devoted six columns of his paper, *The Standard*, to a slashing criticism of socialist "theory" in justification of his retreat from the coalition.

For the situation to have come to a head in this fashion was, as Florence Kelley saw it, a good thing—it stripped George of all pretensions to the role of working class leader. She had never been impressed with his abilities as a theorist, either economic or political; and his tirade in *The Standard* was public confirmation of that opinion.

George himself, when she had visited him a few days earlier with advance sheets of the Preface, had given her all the evidence she needed. In "an especially detailed conversation," she wrote Engels (undated letter, summer, 1887), George confessed

> that he had never looked into Capital and had never *seen* the Condition of the Working Class (I *know* Mr. Lovell sent him a copy) "because I am too much overworked." On *August 6th* he published six columns (Herr Sorge writes me that he sent you the paper) declaring war against the Socialists. The frightful ignorance he displays is nothing new, but the personal confession made to me shows him a

---

[17] FE to FKW, Sept. 15, 1887, p. 192.
[18] Quint, *op. cit.,* pp. 44-46.

wretched humbug. . . . I am delighted that he has been forced, largely by the pamphlet and that conversation about it and the inevitableness of a fair discussion, to define his position. It will make an end of the cant about "common object," etc. and shows once for all the unscrupulousness of the man. He has always dodged discussion before, probably conscious of his own ignorance, but being hard pressed, puts a bold face on it, and . . . gives us six columns of polemics.

Harsh words indeed! But they sprang from her conviction that no matter what George had originally intended, the net effect of his present actions was to confuse, and thereby in a sense betray, the workers who had trusted him.

Having thus dismissed Henry George, she turned her attention to the larger political scene. The presidential elections were only a year away, and Congress was getting ready to debate again the perennial issue of free trade versus protection.

The Free Trade and Protection question is as much in the foreground as ever (*she wrote August* 28) and Marx' Brussels speech of 1849 (*sic!*) (with a preface) would find a ready public. It is the most *timely* publication conceivable, for no American work gives the essence of the Free Trade question as an integral part of the whole system of production as that brief speech does. It contains more than all Mr. George's thick volumes together. . . . I am spending upon the speech all the moments I can steal from my daily hack work and shall send you my translation hoping you may take time to look through it. . . . If necessary I can write a preface but it would be an immense advantage if you would do so, and would raise the value of the pamphlet greatly. . . . It might be well to append some extracts from the Misère [de la philosophie] too, for instance Chap. II, § 1, Siebente und letzte Bemerkung. This reads as if written à propos of the recent moment here, and the chapter upon the nature of "der Rente," in Chap. II, § 4th is in contrast to George's bosh.

To these suggestions Engels replied (September 15) that he would be happy to look over her translation "and compare it with the French original, of which I have perhaps the only copy extant. We will see about the preface later on." The "Seventh *Bemerkung*" he thought most appropriate as an appendix, the chapter on rent "more doubtful."

Writing again on October 24, she now expressed concern as
to how the press might distort the meaning of Marx's speech.
"Of course," she went on, "the protectionist will make the most
of the fact that Marx advocates Free Trade." She urged Engels
to make absolutely clear

> the fact that Free Trade and Protection are really Verwalt-
> ungsmassregeln [administrative measures], and all the
> world treats them as fundamental questions of Social Sci-
> ence—Free Trade or Protectionist Weltanschauung, one
> might say, prevails from the professors and Congress to
> the least of the penny-a-liners.

Then, recalling the difficulties that had followed the suppression of her book of letters on her trip through England, she
added:

> I have my own personal reasons for wishing to have the
> pamphlet perfectly unmistakable on the Protection ques-
> tion, because the Republican protectionist press which is
> all at my father's beck and call will forthwith proclaim
> the fact that the daughter of the apostle of Protection has
> come out in a pamphlet proving Free Trade rank Socialism
> and quoting Marx himself as authority.

Engels appreciated her desire to avoid misinterpretation, but
pointed out that it would really be impossible to answer all
arguments in advance; besides, "a good book makes its way and
has its effect." Nor did he feel, as she did, the urgency for speedy
publication. In addition to the pressure of his many commitments, his eyes were still bothering him; and it was not until
February (1888) that he wrote again, to ask for information on
American customs tariffs and internal taxes to use in the preface. She sent him the material posthaste, with the fervent hope
that translation and preface would be returned in time for use

> before the extreme excitement of the election campaign.
> The interest in the subject will not be so keen again in years
> as it is at present. Indeed for eighteen months or two years
> after a presidential election there is no inducing my
> countrymen to read anything pertaining to the subject
> upon which the campaign turned.[19]

But when the manuscript finally arrived, in mid-May, she
found the publishers far less receptive than she had anticipated:

[19] FKW to FE, Mar. 11, 1888.

The North American Review wrote me through Redpath that "Mr. Rice thought it not advisable to consider the ms.

Mr. Metcalf of the Forum said to me in my own house, "I do not doubt, Mrs. Wischnewetzky, that the article is all you describe. But I cannot afford to stampede my audience." Appleton's pamphlet department said, "The name is enough. We don't want it." Mr. Lovell said of the pamphlet, "Indeed, Mrs. Wischnewetzky, even when you pay all the costs of publication, it's a burden upon any library. I cannot sell ten copies of works of that character." And Lee and Shepard returned me the whole ms. unread.

One man said, "Engels, Engels? Oh! Yes, the man that was hung in Chicago!"

Nonetheless, persistence brought its reward. A second approach to Lee and Shepard persuaded them to reconsider, and they agreed to

have the pamphlet out in first rate shape by August 13th. . . . The pamphlets will sell here to perfection. Lee and Shepard themselves are convinced of it—now that they have *read* it."[20]

To follow her detailed reports of these months is to become aware of a developing philosophy and method of work that came to characterize everything she did in her many areas of interest. Her maxim was beautifully simple: Expose the false, reveal the true. It seemed obvious to her that men and women, when shown the right path, would prefer to follow it—whether in the field of union organization, elections or the socialist revolution. All that was needed was to point the path effectively. The confusions generated by a corrupt press in the control of special interests she would dispel by the clarifying power of scientific socialist analysis. Such analysis must take place not in a vacuum but in a medium of never-ceasing economic and social change.

Thus she was always attentive to the flow of events; at times, indeed, she seemed to view the body politic as a physician views his patient's symptoms, and to prescribe accordingly. Yet the analogy holds only so far. The essential point is that she was always both sensitive and responsive to the need of the moment.

---

[20] Both quotations are from FKW to FE, undated letter, probably July, 1888.

In these years we see her, as a rule, relying on an outpouring of the printed word. Later she would supplement the rush of words with a rush of action. If there is any fault to find, it is that so much of what she knew must be done was done primarily by herself alone. But in the art of recognizing the need and charting the action she was to be one of the best.

CHAPTER VIII

Interlude. A Victory, and a Hurt

With so much the greater portion of her life spent in public service, any description of Florence Kelley as a person necessarily becomes a description of her work. Conversely, an account of her work in effect defines the woman. Perhaps that is why such mention as is made of her, in books by or about her closest friends, dwells less on her physical appearance than on the impact of her personality and the influence of her counsel.

There are, fortunately, a few early portraits of her. Two childhood photographs that appear in *The Survey* show her round-faced and chubby, serious but not solemn, with large dark eyes and dark smooth hair. By the time of her Cornell days she is a tall, erect young woman of graceful carriage, her masses of chestnut hair drawn back from well-shaped ears and fastened in a heavy, braided coil at the back of her head.

In features she seems to have resembled her father more than her mother. Caroline Kelley's face was wide at the brows and curved to an oval cheek and chin. Her daughter even at an early age showed the squarish jaw that became more pronounced as she grew older. In a photograph taken near the turn of the century[1] her eyes are grave and deepset like her father's, her nose is proportioned to her face but, like his, nobly cut; her upper lip is finely modeled, the lower full and firm, and there is the trace of a dimple at the corner of her mouth. Her sons remember her musical, flute-like voice, and colleagues of her later years remark on her commanding presence.

From the first part of the memoirs, too, we can gather that, although not athletic in the modern sense, she did indulge in all the activities deemed proper for a young lady of her era.

[1] In NCL files, Library of Congress, Washington, D.C.

She had learned to ride "on the plains of Wyoming" when she was twelve, and for some years thereafter had her own saddle horse. At Cornell, in spite of her heavy academic schedule, two hours a day were devoted to exercise, and there were other pleasures: "I walked, rode, drove and danced."

As she approaches maturity, however, a curtain seems to be drawn down over the more intimate aspects of her life. This is apparent in the later memoirs, and it is very much in evidence throughout the correspondence with Engels. It is true that the fervor with which she devoted herself to the socialist movement on her return to America left little time for social pleasures. Nor should we expect much personal detail in view of the nature of the correspondence itself. But if we would know how she lived during the first New York years, who her friends were, what her recreations, we must—since no other source is available — scan the letters closely for such few glimpses as she chooses to give.

We do not know, for example, with what resources the Wischnewetzkys arrived in New York, nor what type of medicine the doctor intended to practice. His Würzberg inaugural dissertation was entitled "Some Contributions to the Statistics of Carcinoma of the Lower Lip,"[2] but there is nothing to show that he ever afterward returned to the study of cancer. According to the letters, he left New York in December, 1886, and for the next month was away in Europe. On his return, we read of him mainly in connection with the SLP-Aveling affair and, more briefly, as joint sponsor with his wife of the Preface pamphlet. When, or whether, any patients came at this time is not noted.

At any rate, there seems to have been little financial leeway for the amenities of gracious living. We have no details on what Florence Kelley referred to as "daily drudgery," but it must certainly have included household chores made no lighter by the demands of two babies only sixteen months apart. That she may also have taken on some routine writing job in an effort to add to the family budget is suggested, in the letter from Gloucester, by her reference to "daily hack work." All in all,

---

[2] "Beiträge zur Statistik für carcinoma labii inferiores," Würzberg, Becker, 1886, 23 pp.

she wrote in the same letter, "our life is still a very feverish struggle."

Her third child, John, was born January 31, 1888. Except for passing mention of a "short, sharp illness" the previous fall, there is no hint in the letters of any slowing down of activity before her confinement. There are some charming lines (March 29) about John's "fine christening," which took place at the Sorges' on March 19:

> The Sorge's (who formed the entire company) acted as godfather and godmother, and the occasion was celebrated with the help of a "tüchtige Bowle," the three babies . . . forming a lively and delightful circle of their own.

The Sorges are among the few people mentioned with whom the Wischnewetzkys appear to have been close friends. Florence Kelley's letters show a deep and lasting affection for them. In an anxious paragraph to Engels several months earlier she had described the effect of an enforced absence from Hoboken on the older couple:

> Dr. Wischnewetzky spent New Year's day with our good friends the Sorges and brought away a very sorrowful impression. Both have aged greatly, and grown irritable, take sorely to heart things that cannot be helped, feel horribly unhappy. Mr. Sorge works no less than before, with the difference that his present occupation for which he never had any inclination is utterly repulsive to him now. . . . They are thinking of leaving Rochester and either returning to Hoboken or going somewhere else. But that is a grave matter, because his throat trouble makes his old profession of singing teacher impossible.

And of their return in time for the christening she wrote happily: ". . . they have cheered up since their return to Hoboken to such an extent that they are scarcely to be recognized."[3]

Shortly afterwards, Dr. Wischnewetzky went through "a long and terrible illness." She wrote of this only after he had recovered, and gave no further details at the time. The letter, undated (probably July, 1888), is from her old Philadelphia home address. As to the nature of the visit she is silent, and

---

[3] FKW to FE, Jan. 8, 1888; FKW to FE, Mar. 29, 1888. The Sorges had been leading a lonely existence in a small suburb near Rochester.

there is no mention of her parents. But we have reason to believe that she discussed her many problems with Judge Kelley; and indeed the visit marked the beginning of a welcome reconciliation.[4]

Although regrettably meager in details of a personal nature, the letters of this period were beginning to record interests and activities beyond the narrow world of socialist politics and education. Thus on December 29, 1887, she wrote Engels:

> We see a good deal of some of the more wideawake progressive and influential men among the English speaking organizations (for instance Gompers president of the Federation of Labor with its 600,000 members). He is perfectly fuddled upon the subject [free trade] and so are most of the rest of them.[5]

And in a now familiar vein she had a critical word for AF of L failure to act on matters basic to the welfare of the workers:

> The Federation of Labor held its annual convention in Baltimore a short time ago. It voted in favor of maintaining internal taxes upon cigars; upon improvements in the methods of oyster culture and other equally urgent matters; but of the improvement of the Factory Act, prohibition of the employment of children, etc. not one word could I find.

At this time, too, she had become friends with Helen Stuart Campbell. Some twenty years older than Florence Kelley, Mrs. Campbell was already known as an author of juvenile stories and of a book on home economics. In 1882 she had brought out the first of her works on philanthropy and social reform, *The Problem of the Poor.* Four years later she wrote a series of articles for the *Sunday Tribune* on the working women of New York, which was published in the spring of 1887 as *Prisoners of*

---

[4] Goldmark, *op. cit.,* p. 17.

[5] Gompers recalls the Wischnewetzkys in somewhat kindlier terms: "Among my friends were Dr. Wishnewetski [*sic!*] and his wife well known as Florence Kelly [*sic!*]. I knew them both well and when they made a trip to Europe in the 'eighties' I was glad of an opportunity to share the information they collected." *Seventy Years of Life and Labor: An Autobiography* (New York, 1925), I, 33. Gompers' allusion to the European trip is not quite accurate. Dr. Wischnewetzky did travel to Europe twice that we know of, in December, 1886, and in September, 1888, but he went alone. Gompers probably means "After they had arrived in New York from Europe."

Poverty.[6] This was a sympathetic examination, through personal interviews, not of "cases" but of human beings in distress. "She is good and warm-hearted," Florence Kelley wrote in her December 29 letter, "and gets at everything from the side of strongly human feeling." Mrs. Campbell was planning a trip to England, and "I took the liberty of sending (her) a card to you."

Notwithstanding this widening range of interests, Florence Kelley had been determined all along that she and her husband should win reinstatement in the SLP. In addition to being cleared of unfounded charges, she earnestly hoped the vindication would serve to expose the old leadership and force the installation of a new one.

The September (1887) National Convention should have been the occasion for such a turn of affairs, but this did not occur. The Convention met in Buffalo for four days of sessions, in the course of which substantially the same officers were re-elected. On the last day the delegates took up, among other things, the "Aveling matter" and the "Foster matter." With regard to the former, they voted to uphold the NEC censure of Aveling, but also recommended that, in the future, arrangements for speakers' fees should be made in advance "so as to avoid cases like this." The Foster matter, in the minutes at least, seems to have boiled down to the problem of an unpaid bill ($84.00!) left over from printing *Die Lage*. The Investigating Committee proposed that the Convention disclaim responsibility; instead, the body voted to appoint an arbitration commission of Jonas and Gronlund to settle the question after adjournment.[7] Curiously enough, the Wischnewetzkys were not named in the *Proceedings;* apparently any questions or protests regarding their status were subsumed under "Foster."

---

[6] Roberts Bros., Boston, 1887. The Preface is dated March 3. Florence Kelley cites this work in a footnote in her Philanthropy essay as an illustration of "a law of political economy that the working class receives only enough of the fruits of its labor to maintain itself and bring up the rising generation according to the prevailing declining standard of life of the working class in the given country at the given time."

[7] *Report of the Proceedings of the National Convention of the Socialistic Labor Party:* held at Buffalo, N. Y., Sept. 17, 19, 20, 21, 1887 (New York Labor News Co.), pp. 21, 20. It was this convention that voted to change the name to Socialist Labor Party.

In any event, during the winter the commission did meet to discuss the entire situation with the Wischnewetzkys. The latter stood their ground firmly as to the injustice of the expulsions, and argued their case so persuasively that Florence Kelley could at last write (March 11, 1888):

> The Supervisory Committee, upon recommendation of a com. appointed by the Buffalo Congress, Jonas and Gronlund, to adjust the differences between us and the party, has unconditionally reinstated us, acting over the heads of the Executive and in spite of the frantic protests of the N. Y. section. . . .
> The upshot of it all is that . . . the Exec. is "instrukt Herrn und Frau W. auf ihre Application Karte als einzelstehende Mitglieder auszufertigen"—about as thorough a snub as they could well have earned.

The Executive Committee met this defeat by the unusual tactic of appealing from a higher body to a lower one—the New York section; and the usual tactic of calling for another investigation. They even went so far as to consider a more serious "indictment."

> The protest printed in the accompanying Volksz. of Feb. 25th (*wrote Florence Kelley in the same letter*) originally contained a paragraph accusing us of being agents of foreign (Sozialistischen) powers who are dissatisfied with the American movement and use us as tools to discredit it. Of course it is you who are meant. Jonas did not publish the paragraph. He thinks it will be discussed at the next section meeting.

The charge of "foreign agents" never was publicly made. All that appeared was a brief notice in the *Volkszeitung* (March 31) that the New York section, at a "Sitzung März 2," had declared that it would not readmit the Wischnewetzkys until their accusations against the Executive Committee were withdrawn.[8]

Engels, who had read the notice, congratulated her (April 11) for her success "as far as it goes." Being on the scene, he added, had given her an advantage denied the Avelings, "and thus the

---

[8] It is noteworthy that within a year the division in the ranks of the leadership resulted in the ouster of Rosenberg and three others from the NEC on the dual grounds of differences in policy, and incompetent administration. Rosenberg in particular was denounced for "dictatorial conduct in office, incompetence, dishonesty, and drinking the beer of a boycotted brewery." See Quint, *op. cit.,* pp. 55-56.

hostility to you is reduced to mere local *klatsch,* which with perseverance you are sure to overcome and live down."

It is possible that Engels' prediction would eventually have proved correct. In spite of her battles with the SLP leadership, her socialist convictions had not wavered, and with Engels to cheer her on she was prepared to ride out the storm. What she was not prepared for, however, was a shattering experience she was to encounter later that summer.

The preceding events certainly held no hint. In July she had learned from Sorge that Engels, accompanied by Carl Schorlemmer[9] and the Avelings, was on his way to the United States. The holiday had been planned to give him a chance to rest and recover from his eye trouble. News of the journey had been imparted to Sorge in strictest confidence. "I do not want to fall into the hands of the Messrs. German Socialists," Engels had written on July 11; and had added the admonition that only the Wischnewetzkys were to be notified.

The travelers were met at the dock, with what emotion on Florence Kelley's part we can well imagine. The Avelings stayed long enough for greetings, then went off to attend to their own affairs. Engels was suffering from indigestion, and a heavy cold which Dr. Wischnewetzky diagnosed as bronchitis. Instead of remaining in New York, therefore, and possibly jeopardizing the sightseeing schedule, he and Schorlemmer went over to Hoboken for a few days' rest at the Sorges' before starting out.

The journey through the New England states to Canada, along the St. Lawrence and back through New York State to the city, evoked the keenest pleasure. Engels paid a visit to his nephew Willie Burns—"a splendid fellow . . . exactly the youngster for a country like America"; observed with amusement the contrast between "sleepy Canada" and the "feverish speculative spirit of the Americans"; and relaxed on the slow boat trip down the Hudson. On September 15, four days before sailing time, the party reassembled at the St. Nicholas Hotel in New York.[10]

---

[9] Carl Schorlemmer (1834-1892), one of the early German communists, professor of organic chemistry at Owens College in Manchester, and a member of the Royal Society.

[10] FE to F. Sorge, Aug. 28 and 31, Sept. 10, 11, 12, 1888, pp. 202-205.

Florence Kelley, meanwhile, had gone on to the seaside at Long Branch with the children, expecting to hear at any time that Engels was coming to visit her. But the days went by with no word from her friend, whose trip was now drawing to a close. When a letter finally arrived she could scarcely believe her eyes. On the eve of sailing Engels had written:

I cannot leave America without again expressing my regret that unfortunate circumstances prevented me from seeing you more than once and but for a few moments. There are so many things we should have talked over together, but it cannot be helped . . .

The pain and dismay caused by this inexplicable treatment went deep.

Your note of Sept. 18th is here (*she wrote two days later*) and I can only say that I cannot imagine a keener disappointment than mine that you left America without coming to see me. I could not have imagined in advance your arriving without our being on hand with Mr. Sorge to bid you welcome; and your staying ten days within a two hours' easy ride from us and not taking the trouble to come to see me was a hurt to my feelings which cannot be made good and which there is no use in my trying to conceal.

Engels himself was perhaps not too easy in conscience over his actions, judging by the elaborate explanation and apology he had framed just before leaving, and which he felt constrained to repeat four months later (January 12, 1889)—a letter which she did not bother to answer. To Sorge he blustered a bit in characteristic fashion:

Mother Wischnewetzky is furious because I "was in New York for ten days and did not find time to undertake the two hours' easy railway journey to her . . ."

And again:

Mother Wischnewetzky . . . seems to be hurt by a breach of etiquette and lack of gallantry towards ladies. But I do not allow the little women's rights ladies to demand gallantry from us; if they want men's rights they should also let themselves be treated as men. She will doubtless calm down.[11]

---

[11] FE to F. Sorge, Oct. 10, 1888, p. 207; Jan. 12, 1889, p. 209.

There is more than a touch of male arrogance in this last. One suspects that if Florence Kelley had been a man, an arrangement for meeting might have been worked out. On the other hand, there is some extenuation for Engels' actions—his age (he was nearing seventy), his not too robust health, and his understandable desire to see as much as possible on this one American visit.

But for Florence Kelley there was no extenuation. She sent him the five hundred copies of *Free Trade* he had asked for in his farewell letter, and withdrew into an injured silence which was to last for the next three years.

What effect the rupture as such had on her continuing attitude to the SLP we do not know. There is no evidence either of her resignation or of any further action by the organization. It is possible that, failing the support and encouragement she had drawn from her friendship with Engels, the struggle to recapture her former position lost its significance. Apparently her status as member-at-large stood unquestioned; but with other problems and other interests pressing in on her, the urge —and the opportunity—for party activity would simply have been crowded out.

Yet if the summer of 1888 marked a kind of end, it also marked a beginning—the gradual emergence of Florence Kelley in a new role, that of social reformer. It was a role for which she was eminently fitted, by temperament and by training. It was also one to which she was bringing something new—the conviction, based on her Marxist studies, that poverty and misery were inherent not in the human condition but in the capitalist system. The ultimate need, of course, was to replace the system by a superior one; for this, as yet, there appeared no immediate prospect. But the possibilities were at hand for mounting a series of assaults against the evils rooted in capitalism, and so preparing the way for a socialist society. It was to this radical assault that she would now address herself.

CHAPTER IX

The Assault is Mounted

In a letter to Engels in the spring of 1888, before the unhappy denouement of his visit to America, Florence Kelley had written (March 29):

> I am working up the subject of Child Labor (and compulsory education) using statistics of State Bureaux, State Board of Education Reports, etc. In this volume I shall use exclusively American official data. Later I shall work out a second volume based on European official data for comparison.

Such a comprehensive study would have been a valuable contribution indeed to the field of industrial reform. Unfortunately it was never written, although she continued to collect material for it over the next several years. But a small pamphlet perhaps intended as a preliminary study did appear in 1889. Entitled "Our Toiling Children," it carried on the flyleaf the announcement: "In preparation by the same author, 'Child Labor in the United States'. A treatise upon the historic, economic, social, educational and legal aspects of child labor. . . . To be published during 1889."[1]

The linking of compulsory education with child labor was not new,[2] but for many years the schooling required by any state had been only an adjunct to and a minor restraint upon long working hours. After the Civil War the number of children drawn into the rapidly expanding factory system rose sharply.

---

[1] Woman's Temperance Publications Association, Chicago, 1889. Price 10 cents. The pamphlet was also translated into German and published in edited form in *Die Neue Zeit,* Vol. 7, pp. 168-175, under the title "Die Lohnsklaverie der Amerikanischen Kinder."

[2] As early as 1813, Connecticut had passed a law requiring some education and "attention to morals" for indentured children. But no mention was made of the factory child; and in general the law remained a dead letter. Forest C. Ensign, *Compulsory School Attendance and Child Labor* (New York, 1921), p. 87.

As a consequence, reform groups in many states began to press for more explicit compulsory education laws; at the same time, sentiment was developing to raise the age limit at which a child might start to work. But such laws as did pass were full of loopholes, while enforcement was haphazard or non-existent. In general, the tendency was to rely on compulsory schooling to modify the hours of labor, rather than to prohibit the labor of all children so that they might attend school.

This was the problem to which Florence Kelley now turned. The purpose of her study was to impress upon the public conscience the need to abolish child labor altogether. To do this she had first to establish the fact, against the prevailing notion, that child labor was not the exception, that it was widespread, and was attended by unimaginable horrors. Her second task was to prove that present methods of dealing with the problem of the working child, especially the reliance upon compulsory education as then constituted, were totally inadequate. Her third was to propose a program of action.

She began with the facts—facts as precise as scattered statistics and the nine-year old national census could provide, and as shocking as she intended them to be. In 1880, she wrote, there were 1,118,000 working children between the ages of ten and fifteen. They were in every conceivable industry: glass and electric light works; silk, cotton and woolen mills; rubber, brick and pottery works; manufactories of wallpaper, snuff, cigars, shirts, crackers, baskets—"in short, in every branch in which the application of machinery renders child labor available." When she examined state records, she found little textile workers as young as five years, tenement workers as young as four.

The casualties among the youngsters were appalling, and she documented them: deaths by fire in locked workrooms, by scalding, by drowning in acid vats; maiming of limbs by unguarded machinery; deterioration of health under the strain of incredibly long work-days in unventilated, filthy quarters; daily exposure to all the adult vices produced by poverty and despair.

The laws for dealing with child labor she found "hopelessly inadequate". Although twenty-four states had compulsory education laws, in only one, Massachusetts, was there enforcement. Exceptions made many of the laws meaningless. Factory inspec-

A five-year-old cotton picker who can pick from ten to fifteen pounds a day

Home "finishers": A consumptive mother and her two children

A group of boy miners (some as young as 8 and 9)

CHILD LABOR

A little loom tender

tors ran into unscrupulous employers and desperately needy parents who found a hundred ways of evasion; in six states, inspectors had no enforcement powers at all. Moreover, even if the poverty that drove the children into mill and factory were relieved, she pointed out, the school systems could not accommodate them. For example, there were 10,000 more children in Philadelphia than the schools could provide for, while Albany offered only 12,000 "sittings" for 36,000 children of school age.

Her proposals for legislative remedy were specific and direct. The minimum work age was to be fixed at sixteen, with school attendance made compulsory to the same age. Enforcement was to be carried out by factory inspectors and truant officers, both men and women, amply salaried and provided with expense accounts. There must be enough schools to meet the children's needs.

Her last proposal is of special interest. "Money [should be] supplied by the state through the school authorities for the support of such orphans, half-orphans and children of the unemployed as are now kept out of school by destitution"—in other words, a stipend.

While recognizing the heart of the problem, that "child labor comes of poverty," she does not stop there but traces the whole vicious circle. The low family wages that send the child to work are driven still lower when he enters the factory. He then becomes the competitor of the adult worker, who is finally pushed off the job to join the swelling army of the unemployed. As more heads of families lose their jobs, more children take them, and the cycle is repeated. It is to check this downward spiral, and to protect the living wage of all workers, she notes, that the labor organizations have put forward their own demand for the abolition of child labor and for compulsory education, a demand that so far has met with only indifferent success.

Clearly, the situation requires a new approach, and she has it ready. There is a vast, untapped force at hand, "the mothers, the women of the nation," and she calls upon them to exercise their "efficient persistency" first of all in supporting the demands of the Federation of Labor and the Knights of Labor. Next, where women have the school vote, "they can use it for securing more schools and better ones, and for the enforcement of the compulsory school laws." Where they do not have the vote, they can "petition the Legislature for the care of the children, by the appointment of women inspectors."[3]

She concludes with two specific proposals for action. The first is, to "do as the Working Women's Society in New York has done with great success, organize the working women into Trades' Associations." The second, addressed primarily to middle-class women, is to "abstain from the purchase of goods in the manufacture of which child labor is employed; and . . . make . . . purchases in those stores in which cash boys and cash girls are visibly beyond school age." This latter was a new extension of an old trade union device. Up to then, "selective buying" had been a weapon chiefly of the working class; but, she reasoned, in a good cause it should do just as well in middle-class hands.

The booklet well illustrates what was to be another hallmark of Florence Kelley's work: documentation by an exhaustive collection of facts, combined with concrete, practical programs of action. And these were never arm-chair programs based solely on study, however diligent, but reflected more and more the experiences of real people in a real world.

Thus, her reference to the Working Women's Society called attention to a new kind of movement which was to have a far-reaching influence. The movement had originated in 1886, when a group of cash girls and garment workers began meeting to discuss ways of improving their working conditions. Joined by a number of reform-minded middle-class women, the Society held its first public meeting two years later and announced its objective: "To found trades organizations in trades where they at present do not exist, and to encourage and assist existing labor organizations to the end of increasing wages and shortening hours."[4]

The following year, during the winter of 1889-90, the members

---

[3] In 1888, a bill introduced in the New York State Legislature, providing for the appointment of "not less than six women" as factory inspectors, had been defeated.

[4] The meeting was held Oct. 9, 1888, at 28 Lafayette Place (*New York Times,* Oct. 10, 1888). The objectives of the Society, seven in all, may be found in *Working Women's Society, Annual Report for 1892* (New York, 1893), pp. 2-3.

undertook a careful survey of conditions in retail stores. The survey was presented at a mass meeting on May 6, and made such an impression that before adjournment a resolution was voted to create a committee to assist the Society, by making up lists of shops which "deal justly with their employees," and urging women shoppers to confine their purchases to these as far as possible.[5] By January of the next year, the committee emerged as the New York Consumers League, with its first White List of eight approved merchants.[6]

Just how active a role Florence Kelley was playing at this time—whether she still saw herself as writer rather than participant—is difficult to determine. Her presence is felt, yet factual evidence of any participation is of the slenderest sort. Although her proposal for a consumers pressure group appears unmistakeably in "Our Toiling Children," there is no acknowledgement or mention of her in accounts either of the birth of the New York Consumers League, or of the earlier activities of the Working Women's Society.

There is, however, one curious and unexplained incident which occurred in the late spring of 1889. According to the *New York Times* (June 30), several members of the Working Women's Society, including the then secretary Ida Van Etten, had a "falling out" and "started another organization which has already been incorporated." While not mentioned in the *Times* (or anywhere else previously), Florence Kelley turns up as one of five women signing incorporation papers for a "Working

---

[5] *Report on the Condition of Working Women in New York Retail Stores,* by Alice L. Woodbridge, Secretary, Working Women's Society of New York, Clinton Place, N. Y. Read at the Mass Meeting held at Chickering Hall, May 6, 1890, under the direction of the "Working Women's Society," 27 Clinton Place (New York, 1893). See also Maud Nathan, *The Story of an Epoch Making Movement* (New York, 1926), pp. 15-29.

[6] The Working Women's Society itself scored a victory in the summer of 1890, when it helped secure passage of an amendment to the State Factory Act calling for the appointment of women factory inspectors. Eight women were then named, the first such in the United States. For a brief account of the vicissitudes encountered by the amendment before passage, see the paper delivered by Margaret Finn, one of the appointees, at the Seventh Annual Convention of Factory Inspectors, Chicago, 1893; see *International Association of Factory Inspectors, Annual Conventions, 7-13,* pp. 13-14. New York Governor David B. Hill's veto of, and invitation to rephrase, the original amendment, in *Messages from the Governor,* Vol. VIII, 1885-1891, pp. 837-38. See also Fred Rogers Fairchild, *The Factory Legislation in the State of New York* (New York, 1905), pp. 55-57.

Women's Society of the City of New York." The five were named "trustees, directors, or managers (of) said society," the "business and object" of which was "to promote organization among women engaged in industrial pursuits, and to furnish indemnity to the members of said society by payments of money, collected by way of dues, against losses occasioned by sickness or lack of employment, and also in general to labor for improvements in the condition of working women."[7]

This is all the information we have (Miss Goldmark does not note the incident at all). If a rival organization was intended, there is no indication that it ever functioned as such; nor do the principals in the incorporation appear again as any sort of opposition.[8]

Thanks to the interest aroused by "Our Toiling Children," and by a series of letters to the press on the need for competent investigation of child labor, Florence Kelley was now beginning to attract public attention. As a consequence, she was asked to read a paper at the Seventh National Convention of chiefs and commissioners of labor statistics, meeting in Hartford, Connecticut, the last week in June. She was unable to make the trip, and her paper was read by Colonel E. M. Hutchins, of Iowa, the Secretary of the Convention.[9]

The convention was given full coverage by the *New York Tribune* and the *Hartford Courant* and *Hartford Evening Post*. Both the *Tribune* and the *Post* commented particularly on the heralded presence of Mrs. Wischnewetzky, not only as the daughter of Judge Kelley of Pennsylvania, but also, in the words of the *Post* (June 25), as one "who has devoted her life to social and industrial investigations. She is the author of several important books and is thoroughly familiar with the

---

[7] Certificate of Incorporation (dated June 20) filed in the Office of the Secretary of State, Albany, N. Y., June 22, 1889; Book 15, p. 567/35. The other signers were Ida Van Etten, Frances Morris, Marian Macdaniel and Jane Gillespie. A notice of the incorporation also appeared under "New York Notes" in the *Workmen's Advocate,* July 6, 1889.

[8] In fact, the *Workmen's Advocate* of Feb. 22, 1890, reports that Ida Van Etten had introduced a bill in the Legislature calling for the appointment of eight women factory inspectors, which, if not the same bill that Gov. Hill signed later that year, embodied the successful substance.

[9] The convention was held June 25, 26 and 27, 1889, in the senate chamber of the Capitol. Florence Kelley's paper was read on June 26, after the noon recess.

difficulties surrounding the employment of children." Indeed, the *Post* added, "Perhaps she will be the chief attraction of the convention."

The prediction came close to the mark, for her paper was a vigorous attack on the inadequate compiling of statistics, and the inaccurate use made of whatever figures were finally gathered together. Her first illustration was an analysis of a New York City Board of Health report, which claimed that fewer deaths occurred in tenement houses, in proportion to the population, than in other houses. That claim was demolished, she pointed out, when we discover that the word "tenement" covers not only crowded, disease-ridden slum buildings, but also the finest apartment houses with all sanitary conveniences!

Her second charge was the faulty use made of child labor statistics, especially those brought forward to prove that the number of child workers was decreasing. Her point was that no exact conclusions at all were possible, since in most cases analysis of the figures had not been carried far enough. As she put it:

> Mr. Carroll D. Wright writes me that he thinks child labor is decreasing. I am convinced that it is increasing with frightful rapidity. Neither of us can prove our point, however, because there are, so far as I know, but two statistically perfect statements extant upon this important subject, and one of these does not refer to the question of increase or decrease. Here again it may be well to specify that it is perfectly possible for the sensational horrors of the toil of tiny children to diminish, while the children at work between the ages of thirteen and sixteen are rapidly increasing. . . . The solitary statistically perfect statement referred to, of the movement of child labor, is to be found upon page 1344, vol. 2, Part II of the compendium of the tenth census of the United States.[10]

In these national census figures, the total number of children in the ten- to fifteen-year age group is broken down into working

---

10 *Report of the Bureau of Labor Statistics* (Conn., 1889), p. 43. There is one curious fact about the official record of the proceedings. The volume entitled *National Convention of Labor Bureaus—Proceedings*, 6-8, 1888-1891, omits both her paper and discussion of it. In an apologetic Preface (p. 3), the Convention Secretary related that the paper had been borrowed from him and not returned, and that no other copy had been available. Yet we find a long excerpt, together with much of the discussion by the delegates, in the Connecticut State Bureau report cited above, which is the source for the account presented here.

and non-working children. A percentage comparison of census data for 1870 and 1880 then shows that, on a national scale, child labor has increased relatively as well as absolutely.

As to the "crude" figures made available by the states, Florence Kelley found that "The best State census treatment of child labor is that of Rhode Island for 1875 and 1885." Here the tally shows that even when the age bracket is extended to embrace the seven-to-fifteen-year group, there is still a percentage increase in the number of working children. A simple statistical examination shows that while the population of Rhode Island increased ten percent during the decade, child labor increased twenty-five percent—again a relative as well as an absolute growth.

Compounding the insufficiency and inaccurate use of data, she charged, is the lapse of time between reports, five years in some cases, in others ten. This can lead the public to believe that the conditions reported have been corrected. For example,

> . . . In 1884 the bureau of New York State published a report showing a shocking condition of things. Subsequently factory inspectors were appointed, restrictive legislation was enacted, and as there is no more investigation by the bureau, the public gladly assumes that the inspectors inspect and the restrictions restrict.[11]

One solution, she believed, would be an investigation conducted "simultaneously and persistently" by several State bureaus in different parts of the nation, not of all industries but of certain typical ones. She suggested the silk industry, which was concentrated in the southern New England States, New Jersey and Pennsylvania; the mining industry, with its large component of mine-boys, in the Middle and Western states; and, as typical of southern industry, the cotton mills of North Carolina. And she concluded:

> With the abolition of child labor an urgent demand of every great labor organization in the country, with decrease in school attendance reported year after year by the superintendent of public instruction of New York State, this is certainly neither an inappropriate nor an untimely suggestion.[12]

---

11 *Report of the Bureau of Labor Statistics, op. cit.,* p. 44.
12 *Ibid.,* p. 45.

The defensive nature of the discussion that followed shows how well her accusations had found their mark. Delegates insisted that she was asking for the impossible: "Parents will not tell the exact ages of their children" (Bowditch, Rhode Island); "Labor bureaus are not authorized or equipped in funds to do the type of census enumeration necessary" (John S. Lord, Illinois); ". . . to compare conditions existing in a certain number of establishments at different periods, or in a certain industry at different periods . . . would be unreliable and misleading" (Horace G. Wadlin, Massachusetts); "The factory inspector reports directly to the legislature. . . . Everyone can readily see the impropriety of the Bureau of Labor continuing to pursue the investigation of a subject after a department had been created for that special subject or purpose" (Edward J. Kean, New York).[13]

Of all those present, United States Commissioner Wright showed by far the keenest appreciation of both the paper and the problem. If it were up to him, he said, all children would be barred from factories. As matters stood, he added, child labor in his home state of Massachusetts was in fact decreasing. He referred to Florence Kelley as the "distinguished essayist," and agreed that "the subject of child labor is so important that . . . investigation should be made whenever it is possible."[14]

This admiration for Florence Kelley and her abilities was more than a thing of the moment. Within a few years Commissioner Wright would call upon her to take part in just the type of investigation she was now demanding, and for which her interests, talents and experiences had provided ideal training.

---

13 *Ibid.,* pp. 48-52.
14 *Ibid.,* p. 54.

CHAPTER X

Doors Close, Doors Open

The beginning of the year 1890 brought with it a grievous loss to Florence Kelley, the death of her father. Although Judge Kelley had been in failing health for some time, he had stoically sought to spare his family and friends as much as possible. Unwilling to call attention to his illness in any way, he had not taken a leave of absence from Congress, but continued to attend the daily sessions. He had even given up his customary return to Philadelphia for the Christmas season and remained in Washington, hoping to conserve his strength so as to "hold out until after the holiday" for the sake of his wife and the children and grandchildren. "How difficult," he confessed at the time to his friend Charles O'Neill, "I am finding it to talk much."[1]

Two days before his death he lapsed into unconsciousness. Caroline Kelley was with him when the end came, as were his daughter Harriette (now Mrs. F. Oden Horstmann), both sons, and his secretary H. J. Weirick. On Saturday, January 11, after a memorial service in the House, an honor committee of Senators and Representatives escorted his body to Philadelphia for burial.

Florence Kelley came down from New York for the funeral, which was held the following Monday from her half-sister's residence.[2] But neither in the memoirs nor in her correspondence is there any mention of the death; it was an event she could not bring herself to speak about.

---

[1] Congressional Record, 51st Congress, 1st session, p. 2278. Eulogy by Rep. Charles O'Neill of Pennsylvania.
[2] Philadelphia Public Ledger, Jan. 10 and 11, 1890.

Nor does she refer to a final gesture of solicitude on the part of her father. Except for an annuity to his sister Martha, Judge Kelley left all his estate to his wife during her lifetime. But in a second codicil dated less than two months before his death, he had directed his executor "in his discretion to advance unto my son-in-law Dr. Lazare Wischnewetzky such additional sum or sums of money as may be necessary to complete the purchase of the implements pertaining to the 'Zander system' under his contract with Dr. Zander and secure him possession thereof in New York."[3]

The "implements" represented one more attempt by Dr. Wischnewetzky to establish himself in a paying venture. After recovering from a bout with rheumatic fever—the "long and terrible illness" of the spring of 1888 — he had opened a Mechanico-Therapeutic and Orthopedic Zander Institute for the application of a method of Swedish medical gymnastics originated by Dr. Gustaf Zander. The method employed an elaborate set of some seventy-odd mechanical contrivances—boards, belts, straps, pulleys, weights and springs—for correcting posture deformities and strengthening and improving muscle tone.[4] Yet in spite of the new start, with fashionable offices that began to attract a wealthy clientele, the doctor's own affairs went from bad to worse. There seemed to be no way of escaping the slowly mounting burden of debt; and there was the continuing humiliation of having to borrow to meet daily needs. The legacy may have helped to ease matters for a time, but the relief was only temporary.

Despite her grief and her personal difficulties, Florence Kelley could not for long abstain from the battle in behalf of exploited children, and early that spring she published an article in *Frank Leslie's Illustrated Weekly* on "The Evils of Child Labor."[5] What had always so distressed her in connection with any need

---

[3] Will dated Sept. 20, 1889. Codicils dated Nov. 14, 1889. Will registered Jan. 14, 1890. Historical Society of Pennsylvania, Microfilm, 148, pp. 537-39.

[4] See Dr. Emil S. Zander, "Methods of Medico-Mechanical Gymnastics," in Emil Anders Gabriel Kleen, *Massage and Medical Gymnastics* (London, 1918), Ch. X, pp. 324-69.

[5] March 1, 1890. Excerpts under the title "Child Labor" were reprinted in the *Workmen's Advocate* of March 8.

for reform was widespread public indifference. Now, in her effort to break through this indifference, she spared no details in her account of the horrible slum conditions that drove babies to rag-picking and their older brothers and sisters into sweat-shops and factories.

There is no protection at all for the children of the poor, she wrote, neither in the factories—"We have but one Factory Inspector and he has 12,000 manufacturing establishments under his care"; nor in the schools—"There is no regulation of children by the New York School Board"; nor in their very homes:

> Who ever enforced a law against selling children watered milk? Or sanded sugar? Or infected meat? Or powdered flour? Or rotten fruit? Or decayed fish? Who ever prose-cuted the landlord for murdering children by filth, damp-ness and foul air?

As for philanthropists and the "curious . . . attitude of philan-thropy toward the toil of children":

> The great subsidized charities of the city are huge never resting engines for the promotion and fostering of child labor. The Children's Aid boasts of its 79,000 boys and girls furnished as unpaid "hands" to the farmer of the West during the past three decades. The House of Refuge on Randall's Island is one vast knitting mill . . .

The key to the child labor situation, she emphasized again, was enlarged school accommodations coupled with compulsory attendance; and she noted with satisfaction the recent forma-tion of the School Conference, a delegated body of trade union-ists whose purpose was to urge just such reforms until "the toil of children (is) a thing of the past."

Several weeks later she picked up the question of factory inspection and developed it further. The occasion was an article that had appeared in the February number of the *Nationalist*, organ of a new movement of the same name inspired by Edward Bellamy's *Looking Backward*. Although the Nationalist ideal stopped short of fundamental revolutionary change, the pro-gram of vigorous social and economic reform appealed to Florence Kelley. She was an early member of one of the New

York clubs,[6] and found no contradiction in counting herself both a Socialist and a Nationalist.

The article, "A Footprint in New York," by George N. Miller, praised the influence of the young movement, and cited the beneficent institution of factory inspection as "a genuine footprint of Nationalism." With this Florence Kelley took immediate issue. Rather than a footprint of Nationalism, she wrote in reply,[7] factory inspection is an earmark of Capitalism:

> The factory inspector of today, like the militiaman, is the child of the struggle of labor against capital. The factory inspector enforces the law for the worker against the capitalist, the militiaman shoots down the worker by command of the capitalist.

Nationalists could indeed support the institution of factory inspection, she pointed out, provided they clearly understood that it was neither Nationalism nor Socialism, but a palliative that would become unnecessary when Capitalism was superseded. "It is a far cry from such reforms as these," she concluded, ". . . to Nationalism or Socialism, which proposes to alter [the social] basis and so render palliatives unnecessary."

But such occasional short pieces, and a later contribution to a symposium on "White Child Slavery" in *Arena* (April, 1890), were peripheral activities. Her main attention was still centered on the larger task of collecting and organizing factual material bearing on her major theme. She had extended the scope of her studies, and was now seeking data on the effect of different kinds of industrial work on the health of children of various ages. Once again she was up against a blank wall. Here, interestingly enough, she turned to Richard T. Ely for help.[8]

Ely, a graduate of Columbia and Heidelberg, had been teaching political economy at Johns Hopkins University since 1881, and writing on economics and socialism for almost as long. In 1885 he had been one of the founders of the American Economic

---

[6] The *Workmen's Advocate* of Nov. 29, 1890, carried a report of a meeting of Nationalist Club No. 3, which Florence Kelley attended. For a brief description of the Nationalist movement, see Quint, *op. cit.*, p. 83.

[7] *Workmen's Advocate*, Mar. 15, 1890. Why she did not answer in the *Nationalist* I do not know. Nothing of hers appears in its pages during the three years it was published.

[8] All of Florence Kelley's letters to Ely are from the State Historical Society of Wisconsin, Madison, Wisc.

Richard T. Ely

Association, an organization "designed to promote economic inquiry and to disseminate economic knowledge."[9] While the economics disseminated may have occasionally exhibited a religious tinge—a stated aim of the Association was to develop a system of social ethics—discussion was generally free and non-partisan, and the research monographs published from time to time covered a wide range.

Florence Kelley makes no mention of it then or later, but according to Ely she attended the first annual meeting of the Association in 1886, and we may presume that she joined the Association as early as 1888. The Third Annual Convention was held in Philadelphia in December of that year, and her name first appears on the membership list in the Handbook published the following July.[10]

It was probably in the spring of 1890 that she began to correspond with Ely. The first letter that we have (undated) thanked him for answering "so fully" a previous inquiry as to where she might find certain statistics on the health of workers. Evidently he had sent her, or referred her to, material containing mostly European figures, for she now explained, "What I am especially in search of is *American* data. . . . Except for the N. J. Board of Health Reports I can find nothing." And she went on:

> Would it not be a good idea for some of the graduates of the J. H. medical school to write their theses upon the subject? Could you suggest the matter to some of your colleagues of the Faculty?
> In Europe the investigations in connection with compulsory insurance are destined to throw a flood of light upon the health of the different sections of the working class within the next few years. But we have apparently no source of authoritative information.

She was also, she wrote, lecturing on economics "three times a week before the College Settlement." The lack of economic

---

[9] "Report of the Organization of the American Economic Association," in *American Economic Association Publications*, I, 5.

[10] *Ground Under Our Feet*, (New York, 1938), p. 147. *American Economic Association Publications*, Vol. IV, (1889), Handbook, July, 1889. Florence Kelley's address is listed as "41st and Parrish Sts., Phila."

In a letter to Ely dated Dec. 11, 1890, she wrote: "I wish I could go to the Economic Ass'n Convention [which was to be held in Washington later that month] but I cannot. I mean to submit a paper two years hence." The paper did not appear.

training among college graduates she found deplorable, especially for those "earnest enough in their desire to help solve the social question, to go and live in Rivington St." After a month of "persistent sarcasms" she had been able to prod them into raising money for a very small library on economics, and to arrange their schedules so as to include an hour of daily "systematic reading." But, she added, "The futility of palliative work and the comprehensive nature of the changes going on around us, impress me more from year to year"; and she concluded, "I find myself growing more radical as I grow older, in spite of a temperament anything but radical."

She must have considered Ely sufficiently "radical" to make further discussion with him worthwhile, and to recommend some additional Socialist reading to him.

Do you see the Neue Zeit, published by Dietz in Stuttgart (*she wrote in the same letter*)? A recent number has an extremely interesting onslaught of Karl Marx on the Gotha program of the German Socialists. Engels has held it back all these years and publishes it now because the program is to be remodeled at the next annual conference of the party. There is a great hubbub about it both within and without the party in Germany.

She herself had been a subscriber to *Die Neue Zeit* since her Zürich days, and in her next letter offered to send Ely the copy containing "Engels' criticism of Rodbertus when the Rodbertus furore was at its height in 1884.[11]

For his part, Ely could not but discern that here was a rare and forceful personality, and a mind to be reckoned with. He had written a series of articles for the New York *Independent*, and he now asked her to read them and to let him know what she thought of them. Her answer (undated letter, probably the end of 1890) is notable on several counts. It carries a self-critical confession of a trait that was causing her much concern;

---

[11] Johann Karl Rodbertus (1805-1875), a German economist. The "furore" was over a charge that Marx's treatment of surplus value had been plagiarized from Rodbertus. *Die Neue Zeit* during 1884 replied to the charge with two articles by Kautsky, both titled "Das Kapital von Rodbertus" (pp. 337-50 and 385-402). In 1885, under the title "Marx und Rodbertus," the journal printed (pp. 1-10) Engels' own refutation contained in his preface for the German translation of Marx's *Misère de la philosophie*. Engels extended the refutation in his preface to Vol. II of *Das Kapital* (in English in *Capital*, Vol. II, Kerr edition, Chicago, 1913). The enlarged refutation is dated "London, on Marx's birthday, May 5, 1885."

and it reveals a judicious appreciation of the difference between a cut-and-dried formula for some vague "socialist" future, and a running Marxist analysis of conditions and trends on which to base daily social action.

I shall be very glad to read the Independent articles consecutively, pen in hand (*she wrote*), and shall be grateful if you will send me the full set, as I do not see the paper regularly. But I must warn you that my friends think my criticisms more candid than kindly, and must beg you to make allowances for an inborn brusqueness which has brought me much trouble.

To Ely's request for references to works on agriculture under Socialism, she replied that she knew of none, and could not "see how such a work could very well be undertaken at the present stage."

You see (*she continued*), it is really only the Grönlund sort who undertake to lay down a Socialist scheme at all. The rest of us can only examine the present and past, and try to ascertain which way we are moving and how fast we are going. But we don't venture [to] say how things will be done a hundred years hence, for how can we foresee the technical changes and the discoveries in the domain of applied natural science which may intervene?

The only thing we feel sure of is this, that the minority cannot go on forever exploiting the majority, and that exploitation can be abolished only by removing the means of production from the irresponsible few to the responsible servants of all, and that this can come only when the economic conditions, *and* the intelligence of the masses sufficiently ripen.

In her next letter (February 4, 1891), continuing the exchange of questions and information, she thanked him for sending her some essays, and asked if he knew of any American writers on the hygiene of occupation. "We have a bill in the legislature,"[12] she also told him, "for placing messenger boys and cash girls under the factory acts and reducing the working day of minors to eight hours." Then in an added comment:

---

[12] The Ainsworth bill, drawn up and introduced by the Working Women's Society. It did not pass at the time, but continuing agitation led to the appointment in 1895 of the Reinhardt Commission to investigate working conditions in mercantile establishments. As a result, a law to protect workers in such establishments was enacted the following year; but it expired in 1898 when the legislature failed to appropriate funds for inspectors.

I am interested in watching the preparations for the miners' strike.[13] It seems to me that Mr. Bellamy might flank their movement, if he would, by urging immediate nationalization of the mines.

But the New Nation is not a very vigorous sheet and Mr. B's policy is not very impressive I'm afraid.

In April Ely sent her more material, a manuscript which she referred to (April 23) as "the budget upon Socialism," with the request that she criticize it frankly. This was an early draft of what was to be his *Socialism, an examination of its nature, its strengths and its weaknesses, with suggestions for social reform.*[14] Taking him at his word, she devoted a major part of this and a following letter to a detailed rebuttal of the first chapter, which dealt with the attitude of socialism toward the family. She also, in the second of the two letters, touched on several other points in some of his later chapters.

Ely had undertaken, among other things, to clear up a number of current false notions about socialism, including the charge that it advocated "free love." Of this he made short shrift. But he seems also to have argued that socialism is simply an economic system and therefore, as Florence Kelley quotes him, "entertains no peculiar notions concerning the family as a social institution."

Quite the contrary, she retorted:

> If Socialists may speak for Socialism, it certainly does entertain the notion that the family of today belongs to the industrial system of today; and that its economic foundation, i.e., the economic dependence of the wife upon the husband, passes away with the rest of the economic dependence of one person upon another.

One reference which was fresh in her mind was the *Communist Manifesto*. There Marx (after outlining the case for the common ownership of the means of production) had satirized the bourgeoisie who, as she put it, "having never seen in women anything more than a means of production, . . . forthwith jumped to the conclusion that they, too, were to be held in common."

---

[13] This refers to the strike of the Tennessee Coal Mining Co. employees against the use of convict labor in the mines, a grievance of twenty years standing. The strike began the following April. For a full account, see Philip S. Foner, *History of the Labor Movement in the United States* (New York, 1955) II, 220-26.

[14] New York and London, 1894.

Almost every socialist writer, she continued, has had something to say on marriage as an institution which is molded by the society of the times, and which will change with the times:

> . . . Lewis Morgan's Ancient Society culminates in the inference that the present form of the family is merely transitional.
>
> Engels' Ursprung der Familie des Privateigentums und des Staats hinges upon the transitory nature of the present form of the family.
>
> Bebel's book in the first edition is one continuous broadside fired into the present form of the family.
>
> [If] Morris, Bax and the Avelings . . . may be thought too strongly Marxist to represent English opinion fairly, there is Bernard Shaw with his anti-Marxist Socialism and his anti-marriage-as-it-is-today novels, and Karl Pearson with his morals under Socialism.
>
> Even our own Bellamy both in Looking Backward and in the New Nation frees the wife from the economic thralldom which is the *essential* feature of marriage today.

With the abolition of dependence, she went on:

> there would remain solely inclination and affection to bind husband and wife . . . Today, the duty of providing for beings dependent upon him, determines the life of the average married man; and the duty of providing for her children makes life an endless petty economy for the average wife. And each endures the yoke by reason of the sense of duty in untold numbers of cases in which respect and affection have fled. Hence, if you remove the economic dependence you do make love free.

Several days later, wishing to buttress her thesis further, she wrote again.[15] She had found a paragraph in *Das Kapital* (which she quoted in the original German) in which Marx described the devastating effects of modern industry upon the family. Deplorable as the dissolution of family ties may be, he pointed out, when capitalist industry assigns women and children an important role in production outside the household, it actually creates a new economic foundation for a higher form of family life and of relations between the sexes. And the present "Teutonic-Christian" form of the family need be considered no more absolute and final than the now outmoded Roman, Greek

---

[15] Undated letter, noted by Ely as having been received on April 27.

and Eastern forms. They are all members of an historically developing sequence.[16] This "classic formulation," she asserted, is subscribed to by Socialists

> because they are Socialists and because Socialism involves this view of the family. This idea . . . shows that the transitional aspect of the present family relation is the one which Socialists as such, logically regard as the characteristic aspect. (Her emphasis.)

When we read Ely's Socialism we discover how large a part of his discussion of the family is addressed to her critique. He even quotes verbatim (Page 48) her paragraph beginning "If Socialists may speak for Socialism," although he attributes it only to an unnamed "young American woman socialist." But he sidesteps her argument altogether when he says that she represents merely "a materialist conception of history . . . [which] is, however, no necessary part of socialism." And he quite misconstrues her point about the "transitional form" of the family when he concludes: "Whatever view we take of the evolution of society, it would not seem to follow of necessity that socialism would, if successful, do anything more than purify and elevate the family."[17]

None of this, of course, is any refutation of her position. For the issue between them is not whether Socialism does or does not "elevate the family." On this there is no disagreement. Where they really differ is in their conception of socialism, and, derivatively, of the effect of economic conditions upon social relations.

Basically Ely, although thoroughly read in the history and theory of socialism, stands forth as a Utopian reformer. The socialism he describes at great length is defined so broadly as to wipe out its essential and specific features. In his opinion, an "all-class socialism" was stronger, and therefore more desirable, than a working class socialism[18]—a viewpoint with which Florence Kelley had no patience. "My Socialism is proletarian,"

---

[16] She gives as the German reference, "3rd ed. 1883, Hamburg, p. 506 (of Das Kapital)." It may be found in English in Capital, International Publishers (New York, 1939), I, 496. This is the Moore-Aveling translation, reprinted from the stereotype plates of 1889.

[17] Ely, op. cit., pp. 48-49.

[18] Ibid., p. 179.

she said in the second of the two letters, "and I cannot accept the all-classes-Socialism without so many qualifications as practically to amount to negation outright."

It is perhaps not surprising that of the many points for controversy raised by the Ely manuscript, Florence Kelley should have given most attention to the one on family relationships under capitalism. She had already seen enough examples of home life disintegrating in the endless struggle to achieve a bare subsistence. And there may have been more than a bit of ironic self-portraiture in the picture she drew of marriage cramped, conditioned and squeezed dry by economic dependence, especially of the wife upon the husband.

She had promised Ely that as she read his subsequent chapters she would continue her "epistles of dissent and polemic." But if she did we do not have these letters; and as far as we know it was a full year and a half before she wrote to him again.

For the next months she seems to have been mainly preoccupied with her own affairs. At home, the situation was steadily deteriorating. Yet she did find time and energy to publish one article, "A Decade of Retrogression," in the August issue of *Arena*. This again was part of a symposium, and dealt with the discouraging increase in poverty, crime, illiteracy and disease in New York since 1880, an indictment which she backed up, as usual, with precise and accusing statistics.

Early in October, out of the blue it must have seemed, she received a letter from Engels. The circumstances that prompted him to write were particularly gratifying to her: the London firm of Swan Sonnenschein and Company wanted to bring out a reprint of her translation of *Die Lage*. The terms were good, Engels told her, and he was inclined to accept them as soon as copyright and royalty matters could be settled.

Her pleasure at renewing the old friendship was manifest in her reply, October 13, written in the same lively manner that had marked her earlier letters. She was delighted that "the work of years ago is to come to life again after it seemed for so long a time to be consigned to oblivion." As for the copyright, it was "not, as you thought, in my name, but in that of Rachel Foster, who paid for issuing the book; and the royalty goes to her." There should be no trouble in getting Miss Foster's agreement to republication: "She has married, is Mrs. Rachel Foster Avery and too much absorbed in her two daughters to take much interest in Socialist propaganda."

Then in a rare breakthrough of her usual reserve she continued:

> We have had an atrocious time. After Dr. Wischnewetzky recovered from his rheumatic fever he established a Mechanico-Therapeutic Institute, the most complete one in the world (after examining them *all*) and in an admirable building on Fifth Ave.[19] Almost immediately he counted among his patients Jay Gould, Messrs. Uhl, Ottendorfer and a number more of the same sort. And by irony of Fate, while he was curing the whole company of millionaires we often did not know which way to turn and had nothing whatever for ourselves. After three years of ceaseless struggle, we are hardly better off or more sure of the future than we were at the start.

As for any participation in the SLP, "We have been so absorbed in the struggle for existence for our children and the Institute," she wrote, "that we could do little more than keep an eye upon the organs of the movement."

Even at this date, though, there was no indication that she was contemplating a break with her husband. "I have asked Dr. Wischnewetzky," she noted, "to send you Nos. 1 and 2 of the publication which he has begun, feeling sure that you will be interested in a field of medicine almost untilled by the profession in England and America."[20] And her next letter, November 25, discussed briefly the copyright arrangements, and closed "with kind regards from Dr. Wischnewetzky."

Yet some sort of determination must have been in the making.

---

[19] At 246 Fifth Ave. After moving several times, the Wischnewetzkys were now living at 78 W. 72nd St.

[20] *Contributions to Mechanico-Therapeutics and Orthopedics,* Edited by L. Wischnewetzky, M.D. Published by the Mechanico-Therapeutic and Orthopedic Zander Institute, 246 Fifth Ave., New York City. Price seventy-five cents.

Vol. 1, No. 1, (in the Stuart Collection, New York Public Library) consists of a long preface (pp. 3-21) signed by Dr. Wischnewetzky as Director of the Institute, and an article entitled "The Mechanico-Therapeutic Institute," by Dr. Gustaf Zander, Stockholm (pp. 23-50). The back cover lists the first six issues (Vol. 1, Nos. 1-6) and their contents. Articles "In Preparation" include two by Dr. Wischnewetzky, "The Scientific Status of Mechanico-Therapeutics" and "Mechanico-Therapeutics and Surgery." I have not been able to locate any other issues.

Her last letter to Engels from New York, December 1, was obviously written under great stress:

Dear Mr. Engels,

I received your note of the 21st ult. by the same mail which brought me the enclosed.

The omission of my name is out of the question of course —*or any part of it!* The book is copyrighted with your name as author and mine as translator, and any change would be an infringement on the copyright. . . .[21]

I rely entirely upon your insisting upon this. Yours in haste,

Florence Kelley-Wischnewetzky

What was "enclosed" she did not identify. Nor have we any clue as to why a change in name was suggested, unless in some fashion, perhaps through Sorge, Engels knew of the impending dissolution of her marriage.

There is no sign of the anguish that attended her decision other than the silence with which she cloaked it. But her mind made up, she did not falter. In New York her only recourse would have been a legal separation; she wanted the break to be complete. The laws of Illinois offered her the opportunity for divorce, Jane Addams and Hull House a likely opportunity to work in her chosen field. As the year drew to a close she packed her bags, and with her three little children boarded the train for Chicago.

---

[21] NOTE ADDED IN PROOF: New light is thrown on this paragraph by a recently discovered letter from Engels. ". . . On receiving proof of title page, I found that he [the publisher] had struck out your name on the front and put it on the back in small print . . . on account of that unpronounceable Russian name which he fears might injure the sale of the book, as its bearer surely cannot be expected to know English!" FE to FKW, Jan. 29, 1892. Letter in possession of the Kelley family. What was "enclosed" may have been a copy of the controversial title page.

London 28 Jan. 92.

Dear Mrs Wischnewetzky,

Dear Mrs. Wischnewetzky

1/ The following is an abstract of my agreement with Swan Sonnenschein & Co.

a/ We (that is I in you and Mrs. Avery's name) transfer to them the English copyright of the "Condition" etc.

b/ that they produce it in one volume in their Social Science Series

c/ that they pay us (i.e. you through me) 12½% on full price (2/6ᵈ per copy) 13 copies to be reckoned for 12

d/ the same for stereotype plates and copies sold for colonies

e/ the same on proceeds of copies sold for colonies at reduced prices

f/ that we do not suffer from bad debts contracted by them

g/ that accounts be made up as on 30th June each year and settled within 3 months

h/ that we get 12 free copies

*   *   *   *   *

2/ The book is now printed, out of the appendix I have made a new preface for the British reader. I have suppressed the preface of the Amʳ. edition. On reading proofs I have changed a few expressions, chiefly technical terms, as evident misprints or slips of the pen. As soon as I get our copies I shall send you six of them.

I had another tussle with Sonnenschein, but again had the best of him. On receiving proof of title page, I found that he had struck out your name on the front and put it on the back in small print! Of course I at once protested, and asked Dr. Aveling to see about this, as I could not submit to have the translator, as the party whose simple agent I was in the matter, thus insulted. Of course the man gave in, but it seems impossible to do business with him without having to fight such little tricks. And all this on account of that unpronounceable Russian name which he fears might injure the sale of the book, as its bearer surely cannot be expected to know English!

3/ I shall recount and remit proceeds to you as soon as received every year.

4/ Of course this arrangement with S. S. & Co. put an end to the agency, for this book, of Reeves. I have through the kindness of Dr. Aveling who lives close to Reeves' shop, after a deal of trouble managed to get an account out of him, it amounts to about £5—and also part of the money. There are D 4 [$4]—to be paid yet, but the fellow has caught the influenza just in time to execute delay, so that I do not expect to get it before next week if then, for it is easier to get the truth out of a statesman than a farthing of cash out of Reeves. This settlement therefore must be delayed till my next.

5/ Sonnenschein asked me, would it be right for him to send copies to America? I replied certainly not, for the Amʳ. edition was still on sale, and then I doubted whether you could give him valid permission to do so even if you liked. But I said I would submit the matter to you, and of course in the meantime he does not send any copies.

So, this is I believe the whole budget of news I have to send you today, and as I am obliged to write about half a dozen long letters today, I must conclude.

Yours faithfully,

F. Engels

Full text of letter, F. Engels to F. Kelley-Wischnewetzky

CHAPTER XI

The Social Commitment

Hull House, when Florence Kelley first saw it, was a handsome, many-windowed structure, with wide verandahs set off by stately wooden Corinthian columns. Standing well back from Halstead Street, it dwarfed the inelegant succession of low-storied tenements that had grown up on either side.

The tenements had not entered into the original plans of pioneer Charles J. Hull. In 1856 he had been the first to rear his mansion in what was then a suburban area, hoping that others would follow his example to found a gracious new community. None did, and in a few years Hull moved out. Thereafter the property had been variously used as a second-hand furniture store, a shelter for the Little Sisters of the Poor, and more recently as offices and storerooms for a factory in the rear. With the passage of time and the growth of the city the suburbs were wiped out, and by the middle of the 1880's Hull House stood surrounded by a welter of slums and noisome sweatshops.

Situated thus, the old house seemed admirably located to serve as a center for what was still a new idea in neighborhood aid. The concept of the settlement worker—living in the needy area, knowing the residents and their problems intimately, and on this basis organizing effective relief—had originated when Toynbee Hall was established amidst the slums of London's East End in 1884. Two years later Jane Addams and Ellen Gates Starr, traveling through England, had visited Toynbee Hall and had talked at length with its founder, Canon Samuel A. Barnett. Miss Addams was particularly impressed with the notion of settlement living as a means of communication between the more favored members of society—in this case, the students of

Oxford and Cambridge—and their destitute fellowmen. Such an establishment in her own country, she thought, would be an answer to the desires of many young men and women in comfortable circumstances "to give tangible expression to the democratic ideal," and would serve as an "experimental effort to aid in the solution of the social and individual problems which are engendered by the modern conditions of life in a great city."[1] It was this notion that led finally to the opening of Hull House on September 18, 1889.

Not the first settlement house in the United States,[2] but one made unique by the personality of its founder, Hull House was soon a center and well-spring for a constantly increasing number of activities. Its doors were never closed to any cause, however unpopular. During its first winter, with the Haymarket tragedy still agitating the country, there were "great open meetings every Sunday in the recital hall of the new auditorium," over which the Chicago banker Lyman J. Gage, among others, presided.[3]

Within the neighborhood, the program included classes in English and other subjects, a kindergarten, Boys' and Girls' Clubs, boarding rooms for young working women (the Jane Club), a Working People's Social Science Club, and a Cooperative Coal Association to provide coal at cost to its members. The Coal Association, frankly experimental, lasted only some three years. The Social Science Club, on the other hand, proved hardier. Meeting in weekly debate for seven years, it entertained such a wide range of speakers and subjects, up to and including all the pros and cons of socialism, as to earn Hull House its "early reputation for radicalism."[4]

Still, whatever the standards by which that reputation may

---

[1] Jane Addams, *Twenty Years at Hull House* (New York, 1910), pp. 116, 125. The quotations are from a lecture, "The Subjective Necessity for Social Settlements," delivered by Miss Addams at an Ethical Culture Societies' summer school at Plymouth, Mass., in 1892, and incorporated in the text of her book. The lecture in full may be found in *Forum*, Oct., 1892.

[2] The Neighborhood Settlement, now known as University Settlement, was the first. It was founded in 1886 on New York's East Side, at 184 Eldridge St. College Settlement, also in New York, was opened Sept. 1, 1889 at 95 Rivington St. It is no longer in existence.

[3] Addams, *op. cit.*, p. 178.

[4] *Ibid.*, pp. 79, 134-169, 183.

Jane Addams

Hull House

Henry Demarest Lloyd

or may not have been justified, it is clear that the inspiration for service as projected through Jane Addams drew together an unusual body of workers. Nowhere else, perhaps, could one have come upon so many women of such caliber as elected to begin their careers under Miss Addams, and who then went on to larger service—Julia Lathrop, Grace and Edith Abbott, Mary McDowell, Sophonisba Breckenridge, Dr. Alice Hamilton, and of course Florence Kelley herself.[5]

In the uprooting that the move to Chicago involved, a first concern was to make the transition as easy as possible for the children by finding suitable surroundings for them. As an active settlement worker Florence Kelley would live at Hull House. At the same time, she was anxious to have the youngsters where she could see them easily and often.

With this in mind, before leaving the East, she had taken her problem to Caroline Lloyd, who, with her brother Henry Demarest Lloyd, was visiting New York. Lloyd, originally a law graduate of Columbia, had turned from law practice to journalism, and had gone to Chicago to become financial and literary editor of the then liberal *Tribune*. In 1881 he had made journalistic history with an article on Standard Oil, "The Story of a Great Monopoly," which appeared in William Dean Howells' *Atlantic Monthly* and carried that issue through an unprecedented six reprintings. When the coal operators in Spring Valley, Illinois, some years later shut down the mines in an effort to break the infant United Mine Workers union, Lloyd went into the area to see for himself what was happening. His findings appeared in a book, *A Strike of Millionaires Against the Miners* (1890), that shook up Europeans as well as Americans. Now, with his wife Jessie Bross and their three children, he was living

---

[5] Julia Lathrop: first woman member, Illinois State Board of Charities, first director of Children's Bureau, U. S. Dept. of Labor. Grace Abbott: succeeded Miss Abbott as Director of Children's Bureau. Edith Abbott: a distinguished sociologist. Mary McDowell: first director of University of Chicago Settlement ("behind the yards"), first head of Chicago Branch, Women's Trade Union League. Sophonisba Breckenridge: Dean of University of Chicago's pioneer School of Civics and Philanthropy. Alice Hamilton: pioneer in American industrial medicine and hygiene.

Hull House living accommodations were limited to twenty-five and there was always a waiting list. Dr. Hamilton applied in the spring of 1897 and had to wait six months. The Abbott sisters came later, in 1908.

in Winnetka, some sixteen miles north of Chicago, in a rambling old house overlooking Lake Michigan.[6]

Shortly after arriving in Chicago, Florence Kelley, armed with earlier assurances from "Caro", addressed a brief note to Lloyd, in which she introduced herself as "one of the friends of your sister Miss Caro Lloyd and one of the interested readers of your valuable Strike of Millionaires," and asked for an interview.[7] Lloyd responded cordially, and the resultant friendship was immediate and lasting. The children with their nurse were forthwith taken into the Lloyds' home where they lived for the rest of the winter, "well and happy under Mrs. Lloyd's wise, unwearied kindness," while their mother went to work at Hull House.[8]

Her first job was conducting "a small experimental employment office for working girls and women." With the settlement's facilities already strained, there was no room within the building itself for even a tiny office. Hull House at this time was flanked on one side by a saloon and on the other by a combined morgue and undertaking establishment, and it was in a corner of the latter that Florence Kelley set up shop. Unfortunately, as the memoirs record, within a few months it became clear that "both employers and applicants . . . were too few in the Hull House region to afford a basis for a self-supporting employment office." And while the settlement continued to bring together the job and the worker wherever possible—"from high federal and

---

[6] Caro Lloyd, *Henry Demarest Lloyd* (New York and London, 1912), pp. 19, 41, 59, 61, 124, 135; *The Survey*, June 1, 1927, p. 273. For an excellently detailed and exhaustively documented biography, see Chester McArthur Destler, *Henry Demarest Lloyd and the Empire of Reform* (University of Pennsylvania Press, Phila., 1963).

[7] FKW to HDL, Jan. 4, 1892. The letter is addressed from 161 La Salle St., in care of a Miss M. A. West. There is a small ambiguity here, relative to the memoirs. Mrs. Kelley wrote ("I Go to Work," *The Survey*, June 1, 1927, p. 273): "Thither [to the Lloyds'] Miss Addams convoyed me the day after my arrival at Hull House . . ." But that "arrival" had been placed before the New Year (*ibid.*, p. 271), while the note to Lloyd on Jan. 4 indicates temporary lodgings outside of Hull House as of that date. Perhaps the second "arrival" was the day Mrs. Kelley took up residence in the settlement.

All letters "FKW to HDL" and "FK to HDL" are from the Henry Demarest Lloyd papers in the archives of the Wisconsin State Historical Society, Madison, Wisc.

[8] *The Survey*, June 1, 1927, p. 273.

state offices to rat-catcher"—this was never a self-liquidating enterprise.[9]

A letter to Engels (April 7) gives a significant account of those first months:

> We have a colony of efficient and intelligent women living in a workingmen's quarter, with the house used for all sorts of purposes by about a thousand persons a week. The last form of its activity is the formation of unions of which we have three, the cloakmakers, the shirtmakers and the bookbinders. Next week we are to take the initiative in the systematic endeavor to clear out the sweating dens. There is a fever heat of interest in that phase of the movement just at present. Senator Sherman Hoar[10] is travelling about the country looking into the dens at night and unattended. The Trades Assembly is paying the expenses of weekly mass meetings, and the sanitary authorities are emphasizing the impossibility of their coping, unaided, with the task allotted to them. So we may expect some of the palliative measures pretty soon. . . .
>
> I am living in the colony mentioned above, conducting a bureau of women's labor, and learning more in a week, of the actual conditions of proletarian life in America, than in any previous year.

The "fever heat of interest" had been set off by the appearance early in the year of a pamphlet issued by the Chicago Trades Assembly, exposing sweatshop conditions in the garment industry. The facts had been gathered during the fall of 1891 by Mrs. Thomas J. Morgan (whose husband was secretary of the Machinists' Union and one of the leaders of the Chicago SLP), and the pamphlet created a sensation.[11] Shortly thereafter, Florence Kelley proposed that the State Bureau of Labor Statistics make a formal investigation of the sweating

---

[9] *Ibid.*, p. 272.

[10] Representative (not Senator) Sherman Hoar (1860-1898), Dem., Mass., 52nd Congress (1891-93). On Jan. 17, 1892, Rep. Hoar introduced a resolution that the Committee on Manufactures look into the "so-called 'sweating system of tenement labor'" in "such city or cities of the Union as deemed best," with the power to call witnesses, take sworn testimony and compel production of pertinent books and papers. House Misc. Doc. No. 71, in *House Miscellaneous Documents,* 52nd Congress, 1st Session (Washington, 1892), Vol. I. The results of the investigation were published as "Investigation of the Sweating System by a Committee of the United States House of Representatives, Sherman Hoar, Chairman." Hoar's uncle, Sen. George Frisbie Hoar (1826-1904), Dem., Mass., also served during the 52nd Congress.

[11] *Hull House Maps and Papers* (New York, 1895), p. 43 and bibliography on p. 45; FKW to HDL, June 30, 1892.

system. Her proposal was accepted, and in May she was taken on by the Bureau as a Special Agent—a title she accepted with good grace and no illusions as to the amount of leg-work it concealed.

Writing to Engels on May 27, she described her duties and offered her usual pithy comments:

> As you will see from the heading of this sheet [State of Illinois, Bureau of Labor Statistics], I have been made special agent for the Bureau. I enclose a schedule thinking that it may interest you. For a full schedule, I receive the munificent compensation of fifty cents. This is piece work for the government with no regular salary. It remains to be seen how many I can fill in a month. The greater part of the investigation is now completed and there remain 10,000 schedules to be filled in by "Sweaters' victims" in the clothing trades. They are Poles, Bohemians, Neapolitans, Sicilians and Russian Hebrews, almost excluding all other nationalities.
>
> The work consists in shop visitation, followed by house to house visitation and I find my polyglot acquisitions invaluable. The fact of living directly among the wages earners is also an immense help. The municipal arrangements are so wretched that the filth and overcrowding are worse than I have seen outside of Naples and the East Side of New York. In the ward in which I live, the Nineteenth, with 7,000 children of school age (6-14 inclusive), there are but 2579 school sittings and everything municipal is of the same sort. This aggravates the economic conditions greatly, making possible child labor in most cruel forms and rendering the tenement house manufacture of clothing a deadly danger to the whole community.

From force of habit, no doubt, her letters to Engels from Chicago were still cast in the form of "reports" on the labor and political scene, viewed from her new vantage point. The first few also revealed, with characteristic restraint, the anxieties attendant on the problem of winning a divorce and custody of her children. In her April 7 letter, from Hull House and signed "Florence Kelley," she wrote, "You will see from the change of address and signature the change which has been forced upon my life ... I have cast my lot with the Misses Addams and Starr for as long as they will have me"; and on May 27 she stated simply: "The Illinois courts have now finally awarded me the

FLORENCE KELLEY'S CHILDREN

Nicholas

Margaret

John

custody of my three little children, and I can begin once more to live and act somewhat methodically."[12] It was also possible now for her to set up her own household for the children, "close to the little Winnetka day school" that the young Lloyds attended, and within easy commuting distance of Hull House. It was a good move. "The chicks are well," she wrote Lloyd some weeks later, "and continue to like their new quarters."

Her mind thus at ease, she attacked her summer duties with fresh vigor. Her Bureau work of course occupied her days. At night she taught English at the settlement to a dozen or so eager young immigrants, and in her spare time sought to augment her income by writing. On June 30 she reported to Lloyd:

> In the month from May 23rd when my Bureau work began to June 23rd, I earned $78.00 from the Bureau and $12.00 from the Signal. (They held over so much of my ms. that the payments for the month were only $3.00, $4.00 and $5.00) Nothing came of the Inter-Ocean work for some unexplained reason. However, my current expenses are only $64.00 per month, so that I came out well, so far.[13]

In high spirits she recounted the progress being made by the anti-sweatshop campaign. Chicago had indeed begun to stir uneasily as the spotlight of exposure swept back and forth over the crowded, unwholesome workrooms. A report issued by Commissioner Ware (of the State Health Department), she wrote, had already shamed some of the shops into better quarters. The "Sweating System" pamphlet had been snapped up,

---

[12] Engels reported the divorce in a letter to Kautsky on April 20, 1892: "Mother Wischnewetzky has had to endure all sorts of bad treatment from her husband, has divorced him, now calls herself Mrs. Kelley, and lives with her three children, of whom she has custody, in Chicago." (My translation.) F. Engels, *Aus der Frühzeit des Marxismus*, Engels Briefwechsel mit Kautsky (Prague, 1935), p. 316. Florence Kelley's May 27 letter also thanked Engels for a royalty remittance of " £5, 10 and 6d" from the Swan Sonnenschein edition of *Die Lage*. There are three other references to such remittances in her remaining letters to him: on Nov. 27, 1892, for " £5, 14, 10;" on Nov. 21, 1893 for a small amount transmitted through Sorge; and on Dec. 31, 1894. Of the last she wrote: "These little drafts go a long way towards the children's Christmas presents."

[13] The *Signal*, Champaigne, Ill., is among the "labor publications" listed by the Avelings in the introduction to their *The Labor Movement in America* (*op. cit.*, p. 4). *The Inter Ocean* was a Chicago weekly, that characterized itself as "radically Republican and earnestly American in all things." "The Inter Ocean" in *A History of the City of Chicago, Its Men and Institutions*, publ. by The Inter Ocean (Chicago, 1900), pp. 319-26.

"and a number of people are begging for more." And she continued:

> On Monday morning I told 64 Congregational ministers about our neighbors of the cloak trade. One minister preaches to Henry W. King. He was woe begone when I insisted that H.W.K. is a prop of the system.

Of another prop of the system she commented tartly:

> I had a two hours interview with Marshall Field a week ago. He says he cannot deprive worthy widows of the chance of working at home with their children. The only one I have yet found working for him, earned $9.37 *in 13 weeks* and we fed her children meanwhile! (*Her emphasis.*)

As matters stood in that summer of 1892, not just Chicago but the entire state of Illinois was in a mood for change. The first faint tremors of what was to be next year's panic and depression were beginning to be felt. Spurred by prolonged distress in the agricultural states, the Populist movement had grown to a stature that demanded respectful recognition by the major parties. The nomination of John Peter Altgeld as the Democratic candidate for governor of Illinois was a political expedient for the party. For labor and the friends of labor it was a political triumph. Altgeld was already known as an advocate of legislative and labor reforms, including the eight-hour day and abolition of the sweatshops. During his campaign he stumped the state from end to end, lashing out at the trusts and declaring the workingman's right to organize and strike. He made enemies, he almost ruined his health, but he won the election.

There are no letters of Florence Kelley's during the campaign period, and so we have nothing to indicate her views on the candidate at the time.[14] Some correspondence may have been lost; more probably, she was simply too busy to write. In addition to all her other duties, she had taken on a number of speaking engagements in Chicago and neighboring areas. Now the late summer brought a new demand on her energies.

---

[14] In the memoirs she recalls Altgeld with appreciation and esteem: "He was a somber figure. The relentless hardships of experience as a boy and youth had left him embittered against Fate and against certain personal enemies, but infinitely tender towards the sufferings of childhood, old age and poverty." *The Survey*, June 1, 1927, p. 274.

In July Congress had instructed the United States Department of Labor, under Commissioner Carroll D. Wright, to make a national investigation of city slums. Sixteen cities including Chicago were designated, and preliminary studies ordered. Remembering the impression Florence Kelley had made with her paper at the Hartford convention a few years earlier, and no doubt aware of her activities as an agent of the Illinois State Bureau, Wright sought her out to work on the preliminary study for Chicago.[15]

Thus plunged once more into a daily round of painstaking inquiry, it is not until late November, in a letter to Lloyd, that we hear of the rapid pace she was maintaining:

> I have swarmed off from Hull House into a flat nearby with my mother and my bairns . . .
>
> I am teaching in the Polk Street night school Monday to Friday evening inclusive. By day I am a "temporary expert" in the employ of the Department of Labor—Carroll D. Wright—and, on Dec. 4th (Sunday) I go to Geneva, Dec. 11th to Madison to tout for Hull House under the auspices of Mr. Ely, and Dec. 17th and 18th to Oak Park to speak on Hull House and the Sweating System on Sat. and Sunday eves.
>
> Me voila! There is only a limited amount of me at best; and, such as it is, it works twelve hours on weekdays for "grub and debts" and on Sundays it goes out of town to tell the outlying public how life looks in the Nineteenth.
>
> By way of consoling the small fry for these absences I take one with me. Puss [Margaret] is going to Geneva and Ko [Nicholas] to Madison with me.[16]

A letter to Engels at about the same time (November 27) also referred to her teaching:

> I have sixty pupils, Greeks, French, Germans, Austrians, Poles, Russians, Bohemians, dividing the work of teaching them with a German American lady who has the more advanced pupils . . . There is one family in which father,

---

[15] These surveys showed that the $20,000 appropriated for the study was totally inadequate. Accordingly, the number of cities for intensive study was cut to four: New York, Philadelphia, Baltimore and Chicago. The "government schedule men" came into Chicago in April, 1893, and worked under Florence Kelley's supervision.

[16] FK to HDL, Nov. 28, 1892. Ely had written her in the fall about arrangements for a speaker from Wisconsin to participate in a Hull House lecture series, and at the same time invited her to Madison. She answered him Oct. 5. This was probably the first exchange since she left New York.

mother, two adult sons and a little daughter are all at work side by side over their first readers. They are recent immigrants from Bohemia.

In this letter she referred again to a phenomenon which had troubled her over the years—that in the United States at least, socialism as a theory and an ideal appealed to the middle class rather than to the workers. She had touched on it in her April 7 letter: "So far as my limited observation goes, I find more 'root and branch Socialism' among men and women of the prosperous class than I do among our native . . . wages earners." Now she wrote at greater length:

> The increased discussion of socialism here is very marked, though the study of books and requests for lectures come almost exclusively from people of the prosperous middle class. Thus I have been asked to speak twice before the Secular Union and five times in churches in Chicago and its suburbs, and the more radically I speak the more vigorous the discussion in all these meetings. But in the workingmen's meetings, Socialists are regarded as bores, nuisances and professional promoters of discord, not only between workingmen and capitalists, but especially among workingmen. And certainly the local Socialist agitators, Morgan and the Germans, faithfully earn the dislike with which they are regarded.

By her reference once again to the contrasting responses to radicalism, as between workers and liberals, she reveals some still unresolved questions in her own political outlook. She could be quite aware, in arguing with Ely, of the variegated theories put forward in the name of socialism, and take her own foursquare stand with the "proletarian Socialism" of the Marxists. But she found it puzzling and disappointing that those who stood to benefit most from social change seemed generally to show the least interest in the movement that was to bring it about.

One of the reasons for disinterest she rightly identified: in Chicago, as in New York, the socialists were a small sectarian group still trying to reach and influence American workers in alien terms spoken for the most part in an alien tongue. But this was only one reason, and it left unanswered the further questions of *why* the exploited worker does not more quickly grasp the circumstances of his exploitation, and *why* he does not hasten to ally himself with the organization dedicated to his liberation. It is not that she failed to answer such questions—they have not been answered wholly as of this late date—but that up to now she had not really come to grips with them.

On the other hand, it is not surprising, in the context of the times, that the "prosperous middle class"—actually the liberal sector of that class—should have exhibited interest in and even responded to the appeal of socialism as a theory. The response had assumed its most organized form in the fusion of a traditional Christian concern for the underprivileged with Utopian Socialist solutions, to form the new movement known as Christian Socialism. This movement Florence Kelley had already discounted as altogether vague and indeterminate. She was in fact still attempting to assemble her own ideas as to the necessary elements of an indigenous American socialism; but she was not yet ready to formulate them. For the present it was enough to "speak radically" to whoever would listen.

With the echoes of Altgeld's election victory still vibrating across the state, the Illinois Legislature opened its thirty-eighth session on January 4, 1893. By this time public concern over sweatshop conditions could no longer be ignored. Shortly after the opening gavel fell, the General Assembly of the Legislature appointed a Joint Special Committee of the Senate and House of Representatives of Illinois to make their own survey, and accepted the offer of Florence Kelley and another Hull House resident, Mary E. Kenney, to guide the commissioners through the district.

> The Commission had been intended as a sop to labor and a sinecure, a protracted junket to Chicago, for a number of rural legislators. Our overwhelming hospitality and devotion to the thoroughness and success of their investigation by personallly conducted visits to sweatshops, though irksome in the extreme to the lawgivers, ended in a report so compendicus, so readable, so surprising that they presented it with pride to the legislature. . . . For the press the sweating system was that winter a sensation. No one was yet blasé.[17]

17 *The Survey, op. cit.,* p. 273.

The report was published March 1, and resulted in the introduction of a bill which was a milestone in protective and restrictive legislation in Illinois. It created a state factory inspection department with powers broad enough to permit the confiscation and destruction of garments manufactured in homes where contagious diseases were found; set up strict sanitary standards for home workshops where articles of clothing, artificial flowers or cigars were made or finished; required owners of sweatshops to furnish, on demand, lists of names and addresses of contractors and workers; and most important, since there had been no previous effective restriction, set an eight-hour work day for women, girls and children, with fourteen the minimum age at which children might be employed "in any branch of manufacture." For children between the ages of fourteen and sixteen, an affidavit of age was required from the parents or guardian, and one certifying the child's physical fitness from a physician.[18]

As soon as the bill was introduced, a campaign for its passage went into high gear. All elements of the community were enlisted —the trade unions, the churches, benefit societies, social clubs, and dozens of men and women of no particular affiliation but of high enthusiasm. Henry D. Lloyd and the Hull House members, led by Jane Addams and Florence Kelley, worked heroically, speaking night after night wherever meetings could be organized. By day they joined the groups of lobbyists who besieged the state capital, and who ranged from trade union committees to members of the newly formed General Federation of Women's Clubs.

One unexpected factor in the campaign was the "suspiciously little opposition in the press or the legislature" while the bill was pending—probably because no one except the bill's supporters took it seriously. As Florence Kelley noted later in the memoirs, Illinois had a long record of indifference to law enforcement. In addition, there were almost no labor statutes on the books to enforce. The only child labor law was a Chicago city ordinance which prohibited work under the age of ten, and waived that prohibition if the child had a dependent adult

---

[18] These first eight sections of the Factory and Workshop Inspection Law are found in *Illinois—Factory Inspector's Report,* 1894 (Springfield, Ill., 1895), pp. 8-9.

relative! Such social legislation as did manage to slip through was likely to be ignored, declared unconstitutional by the State Supreme Court, or repealed by the next Legislature.[19]

But whatever may have been the reasons, opposition remained minimal; and backed vigorously by the new governor, the bill moved smoothly through its successive stages. On June 7 Florence Kelley wrote exultantly to Ely:

> Our "Anti-Sweat Shop" bill passed the Senate without a dissenting voice, and yesterday passed second reading in the House, and comes up next week in the House for a final (3rd) reading. The Governor has promised me to sign it, and he will appoint a hard-working inspector. By next year this time the long hours and unsanitary conditions will be a thing of the past.

While her longer range forecast erred on the side of optimism, her immediate hopes were more than justified. The bill went through the Illinois House as easily as it had passed the Senate, and on July 1 Governor Altgeld signed it into law. He first offered the Chief Inspectorship to Lloyd, who declined it and suggested Florence Kelley. Altgeld took the suggestion.[20]

---

[19] *The Survey, loc. cit.*
[20] *Ibid.*

CHAPTER XII

Chief Factory Inspector of Illinois

To have had thus suddenly placed in her hands the actual power to do battle in defense of defenseless children, filled Florence Kelley with great joy and a deep sense of obligation. On July 13 she wrote to Lloyd:

> Governor Altgeld made my boy a good birthday present without knowing it when he mailed yesterday the commission which assures us four years of permanent useful employment. I only hope I may have the insight to make the most of the huge opportunity he has given me.

It needed a good deal of ingenuity as well as insight to take advantage of the opportunity, in spite of an excellent assistant inspector in the person of Alzina P. Stevens, and the six men and four women deputy inspectors. The Illinois legislature had allocated a mere $12,000 annually for the new department, "to cover salaries, traveling expenses, printing, court costs and rent of an office in Chicago." The Chief Inspector's salary was $1,500, the Assistant Inspector's $1,000, while the deputy inspectors drew $720 each. "Needless to say," the memoirs commented dryly, "this had been voted by a legislature predominantly rural."[1]

The choice of Mrs. Stevens as assistant was an especially appropriate one. A trade unionist and one-time member of the Knights of Labor, she had for many years recognized the multiple problems and dangers attached to child labor. At the age of thirteen she had gone to work in a cotton mill in New Hampshire; had seen a young girl friend step unsuspectingly into an unguarded elevator shaft and be dashed to death; had herself lost a right index finger as she attempted to clean behind her loom while it was running,

---

[1] *The Survey, op. cit.,* p. 274.

because the looms were running ten hours a day and to clean when the looms were stopped meant going into the mills before 6:30 in the morning. . . . I was taken to the corporation doctor, whom the corporation employed to lump its accident cases at so much a year, and he gave me, presumably, so much or so little attention as was my pro rata share under this lump arrangement. It was not enough to save the worst injured of my fingers, and mortification having set in he proceeded to cut the finger off in what sur- geons have since told me was anything but a workmanlike way. Two weeks of physical suffering, and mental suffering even greater (for I feared I had lost the use of the hand on which my livelihood depended) had unfitted me for an anesthetic. The doctor mixed a glass of whiskey and water and offered me that, and when I declined it, the second hand of the mill, who accompanied me to the doctor's office— the corporation did not furnish a nurse—said he would drink the whiskey and I could smell his breath. He drank the whiskey and the doctor sawed off the finger and I watched both operations.[2]

The appointment of two such dynamic personalities did not go unremarked.

A legend exists (*wrote Julia Lathrop many years later*) that when the announcement of these two appointments was made someone remonstrated in a friendly way, saying that two such "big women" would never be able to work together, to which the governor replied, according to the legend, "If they are big enough for the job, they will get along together well enough." The event proved the governor was right.[3]

The Chief Inspector lost no time in getting to work. Three days after the appointment was made she called her staff to- gether to lay out a program of action. For twelve people with a limited budget the most careful planning was necessary. Only in Chicago, thanks to the slum and sweatshop investigations, was any information already at hand; the rest of the state was a statistical blank. "The law and the inspectors being alike un- tried," wrote Florence Kelley in her first Factory Inspector's Report, "the first three months were spent in ascertaining where

[2] "Child Labor," paper read by Mrs. Alzina P. Stevens at the Seventh Annual Convention of Factory Inspectors, Chicago, Sept. 19-22, 1893. In *International Association of Factory Inspectors of North America* (Proceedings), pp. 46-47.
[3] Memorial tribute to Florence Kelley, in *The Survey*, Mar. 15, 1932, p. 677.

women and children are employed in factories and workshops, and in making known the provisions of the law to employers and employed."

She also obtained a ruling from State Attorney-General Moloney early in August that the law was "general in application," and that no industry or manufacturer was exempt.[4] "The papers are so savage in their onslaught upon us," she wrote Ely on August 20,

> that I think we must be doing fairly good work. We have had no prosecutions yet under the new law, of which I enclose a copy; but I am preparing for a long series of them to begin next week and continue for a month or more. Meanwhile the large manufacturers are obeying promptly and the little employers are bumptious just in proportion to the badness of their shops.

Some of the employers were more than bumptious. The story is told that on one of her early inspection trips, Florence Kelley was the target of a sniper's bullets, which fortunately missed their mark.[5]

One immediate result of the legislation, even before prosecutions began, was the discharge of a number of boys and girls under fourteen from the "sewing, metal-stamping, wood-working, book-binding, box, candy, tobacco and cigar trades." Faced with enforcement powers that made violation of the law a misdemeanor subject to fine, manufacturers were quickly persuaded to require affidavits of age from children applying for work. And parents, unwilling to commit perjury, also proved generally cooperative.[6]

To reinforce the section providing for health certificates, a free examination center was set up, to which working children "markedly undersized, . . . diseased or deformed" could be referred by the Inspector's office. The center was headed by Dr. Bayard Taylor Holmes, of the College of Physicians and Surgeons (later the Medical Department of the University of Illinois), and Dr. Josephine Milligan of Hull House. It was staffed by Dr. Holmes' students, who ran each child through a

---

[4] *Illinois—Factory Inspector's Report,* 1893 (Springfield, Ill., 1894), p. 7.

[5] Mr. Augustus M. Kelley, Mrs. Kelley's grandson, recalls being told of this incident when he visited Hull House in the summer of 1932.

[6] *Factory Inspector's Report,* 1893, *op. cit.,* p. 8.

series of tests "with no other reward than a widened knowledge of the physique of children of the wage earning class."

The examination center was an important adjunct to the Inspector's office, as well as an innovation. "There is so far as is known to the inspectors," Florence Kelley wrote in her First Report, "no public physician or body of medical men to whom children can be sent for careful examination free of charge." It was no secret that the affidavits furnished by company doctors were often totally unreliable; so were those handed out by so-called physicians, who made a good thing out of it by charging anywhere from fifty cents to two dollars for worthless certificates.[7]

A classic example was the case of a "delicate-looking little girl" who worked in a tailor shop, and was found by the inspector to be rachitic and to have a bad spine curvature. Ordered discharged, she turned up a few days later in the same shop with a certificate, "signed by a physician in good standing," which read:

> This is to certify that I examined Miss Annie Cihlar, and found her in a physiological [sic!] condition.

For accepting the certificate the employer was brought into court as a test case, convicted and fined. The child then went to another doctor, who declared her "well developed for her age," and in his opinion perfectly healthy.

> The muscles of the right side of the trunk (he added) are better developed than upon the left side, which has a tendency to draw spine to that side, as a result of greater muscular activity upon that side. I cannot find no desease [sic!] of the spine.

By this time the employer had learned his lesson, submitted the certificate to the inspector, and made no protest when it was rejected.[8]

The story of Annie Cihlar is not unique. Hers was but one of the many instances of work-induced deformity in children with which the Factory Inspector's Reports are studded. These examples, however, were never intended to be stacked away on neglected shelves, but were to be used publicly as additional

---

[7] Ibid., p. 10.
[8] Ibid., pp. 9-10.

ammunition against child labor. As Florence Kelley wrote Lloyd on October 10:

> We are weighing and measuring children at a great rate and shall publish photographs of deformed children in the cutlery trade, where every boy yet found has shown the same deformity of the right shoulder. . . . I think the medical chapter of this report will start a new line of activity for medical men and factory inspectors both.

Indeed, as the work went on, the need for publicity in all areas became imperatively clear. There was, the inspectors found, a sickeningly high incidence of mutilation, among adults as well as children, from dangerous and unguarded machinery. The law did not provide for inspection of machinery, nor did it give the Chief Inspector the power to order safeguards. "Nowhere in the civilized world," she wrote in her 1894 Report (p. 26), "has it been made a crime to endanger life and limb of employees in a factory or workshop by failure to supply safeguards." In this Report and the two that followed (1895, 1896), she urged repeatedly that the Factory Act be so amended as to make it possible to prosecute criminally for such failure.

Still, with the full weight of the Governor's office behind it, the new law, limited as it was, did have an impact on many sections of the community. The Board of Education agreed to supply truant officers to see that the several hundred children ordered out of the factories went into the schools instead of the streets. The Illinois Federation of Women's Clubs cooperated in raising "scholarship" funds to be paid over to families in cases where the child's wages were actually needed to keep the family from starving, the child then attending school until he reached the legal working age.[9] Even some of the newspapers took a more favorable tone. "The Herald, Inter-Ocean and Record are all cooperating now, satisfactorily," Florence Kelley informed Lloyd in her October 10 letter.

While the Chief Inspector and her cohorts with their slim resources were working small miracles in the industrial jungle, a miracle of another sort, lavishly nurtured, had come into being

---

[9] "Wage Earning Children," Florence Kelley and Alzina P. Stevens, in *Hull House Maps and Papers*, p. 53; Florence Kelley, *Some Ethical Gains Through Legislation* (New York, 1905), p. 41.

on the outskirts of the city. A World's Fair to celebrate the 400th anniversary of the discovery of America had been the subject of excitement and rivalry for several years. With a number of cities bidding for the honor of housing this Columbian Exposition, Chicago had won out, and early in 1892 had set to work converting a swamp on the south side of Lake Michigan into Fair grounds.

The fabulous "White City" of gleaming stucco and light, rising at the water's edge, stood in challenging contrast to the industrial grime of the surrounding area. As Florence Kelley had written Engels in her May 27 letter:

> . . . when all the world and his wife come to look at the Fair, they will see the richest, filthiest, ugliest aggregation of houses, streets and people to be called a city, that Carlyle's worst dyspepsia could have conjured up.

But as the grand design of the Fair began to take shape, she too fell under the spell of "that marvelous achievement of art, architecture and enterprise unified for a common, noble purpose." By November she was writing Engels:

> The Fair, next year, will be magnificent in its scope and beautiful in location and buildings. I have seen several World's Fairs, but never anything comparable to the beauty of the City by the Lake which has sprung up, as if by magic, during the past year. I hope you may come to see it, and if you do, come early, not later than June 15 here in Chicago; for the crowds and the weather in August and September will be intolerable.

Hers was not the only such invitation. Several months later (February or March, 1893) Lloyd wrote to ask if Engels could read a paper at the International Labor Congress to be held that September in connection with the Fair.[10] Engels replied that, tempting as the offer was, he was completely absorbed in the last stages of editing Volume III of *Kapital*, "which ought to have been out years ago," and could not possibly spare the time for a paper "which ought not to be a journalistic commonplace . . . [but] the very best I can furnish." As a "small con-

---

[10] Lloyd was chairman of the committee on Program and Correspondence for the Congress, which was held under the auspices of the Chicago Trades and Labor Assembly August 29 to September 4, 1893. Keir Hardie and Sidney Webb were among the foreign visitors. C. Lloyd, *op. cit.,* I, 162-63; Destler, *op. cit.,* p. 259.

tribution" to the Congress he sent Lloyd copies of the *Communist Manifesto* and *Socialism, Utopian and Scientific*.[11] Lloyd knew Engels personally, having interviewed him in London in the summer of 1891,[12] but the idea of inviting him may well have come from Florence Kelley. And there must surely have been a twinge of the old disappointment when his answer came back and she realized that not even the Fair and the International Labor Congress could persuade him to cross the Atlantic again.

Memorable as it was for its displays of all the best in human ingenuity and invention, the Fair was also to be unhappily remembered for the smallpox epidemic that followed. As far as can be determined, the epidemic started with a single case, later traced to the Midway of the Exposition but presumably hushed up at the time so as not to affect attendance. By the close of the Fair a number of cases had been reported among West Side garment workers, and by the beginning of 1894 the total had reached alarming proportions.

The appearance of the disease among sweatshop workers brought the situation legally within the mandate of the Factory Inspector's Office. But it was one thing, in the ordinary course of events, to search out unsanitary quarters and have them cleaned up; or, finding evidence of contagion in a single tenement workshop, to order the contaminated products burned. It was quite another to be confronted with an epidemic so severe as to demand the closest attention of the Board of Health and the serious concern of the entire City Administration. There was also some question as to the measure of protection to be gained by locating infected garments and either sterilizing or destroying them. Still, this at least was within the competence of Florence Kelley and her deputies, and they set about it, although the difficulties proved almost overwhelming.

There was first of all the sheer size of the task—examination of "between 950 and 1000 shops and about 25,000 other rooms in which garments are manufactured." The daily sick lists issued by the Board of Health, which should have served as guides to

---

[11] FE to HDL, [March, 1893], *Letters to Americans*, pp. 251-52 and note p. 151. In return, Lloyd sent Engels a copy of his own *A Strike of Millionaires Against the Miners*. FE to HDL, May, 1893, in C. Lloyd, *op. cit.*, I, 135-36.

[12] Destler, *op. cit.*, p. 249.

inspection, were far from complete, and had to be supplemented by reports of district physicians, when and wherever obtainable. "Requests [to the Board] for immediate vaccination . . . produced no results." The yellow smallpox placard was often torn down, posted obscurely or simply ignored. Tradesmen continued to come and go freely among the tenements, and tenement residents went about their business as usual.[13]

Older immigrants who had survived smallpox in their home countries or had been vaccinated on arrival were relatively safe, but among the children the casualties were very great. Added to the high mortality of the disease itself was the reluctance of parents to admit that a child was ill. Fearing vaccination, fearing hospitalization, ("Parents dread to see suffering little children carried away to a pest-house where seventy percent of all the patients die"), they resorted to all sorts of subterfuges—hiding children in closets or in burlap coffee bags, wrapping them in cloths to resemble bundles of garments and smuggling them to other parts of town, locking doors and dousing lights so that even the neighbors would think the family had gone away.[14]

The manufacturers, for their part, refused to recognize the necessity for stringent measures, and stubbornly resisted official orders to destroy garments or not to give them out for finishing in infected areas. The Illinois Manufacturers Association, formed early in 1893, suddenly came to life with a series of letters to the tenement garment workers promising protection against "molestation" by inspectors who, the Association declared, were operating under an obviously unconstitutional law.

Finally on May 10, 1894, Governor Altgeld called together representatives of the Boards of Health of Michigan, Wisconsin, Illinois, Ohio and Indiana, to meet with the Chicago garment manufacturers. The Illinois Inspector's Office recommended a six-months suspension of all tenement house work and the transfer of work to suitable factories where controls could be maintained. The manufacturers rejected this as impossible, and offered instead a watered-down resolution that was even less

    [13] *First Special Report, Smallpox Epidemic* (Illinois, 1894), pp. 5-7; *The Survey, op. cit.*, p. 274.
    [14] *First Special Report*, p. 40.

Gov. John Peter Altgeld

effective than the Factory Act provision. However, a threat by the Governor to ask the states bordering on Illinois to embargo all needle trades products shipped out of Chicago finally convinced the manufacturers that the law must be obeyed. The City Board of Health set up a public sterilizer; a program of vaccination was instituted in good earnest; and "from this time the removal of patients to the pest-house and the fumigation of infected premises was somewhat expedited."[15]

Whatever the epidemic may have taught the people of Chicago, to Florence Kelley the lesson was exceedingly clear: ". . . the impossibility of guaranteeing safety for the purchasing public as long as tenement house manufacture is permitted."[16] To the familiar plea that such manufacture "affords cheaper garments than could be produced in any other way," she retorted:

> . . . This is a mere assertion, which cannot be proved until an experiment has been made in manufacturing upon a large scale and in factories equipped with electricity or steam. . . . But even if the assertion were true, the cheapness of the garments would be a poor compensation to the Nation for the continuous dissemination of disease, and the degradation of an industry employing tens of thousands of people.[17]

Unfortunately, neither her logic nor her idealism evoked a perceptible response. Although she continued to press her argument during the remainder of her term as Inspector, and later in a widened field as General Secretary of the National Consumers League, almost two decades would pass before the first mild laws against home manufacture were finally upheld.

If one part of the Chief Inspector's duties was to seek out and publicize illegal working conditions, another was to enforce the law against those responsible for such conditions. An early obstacle to enforcement, however, had arisen in the person of the Cook County district attorney himself. Florence Kelley tells the story in the memoirs.

A short time after taking office she had gone to this "brisk

---

[15] *Ibid.*, pp. 8, 9; *The Survey, op. cit.*, p. 301.
[16] *First Special Report*, p. 5.
[17] *Illinois—Factory Inspector's Report*, 1895 (Springfield, Ill., 1896), p. 57.

young politician" with complete evidence against an employer
who had hired an eleven-year-old to gild picture frames. The
boy's right arm had become paralyzed from the poisonous fluid,
and the Inspector's office was ready to prosecute. Not so the
district attorney. "Don't count on me," he had said. "You bring
me this evidence this week against some little two-by-six
picture-frame maker, and how do I know you won't bring me
a suit against Marshall Field next week? I'm overloaded. I
wouldn't reach this case inside of two years."[18]

That was enough for Florence Kelley. She went straight from
the district attorney's office to the Law School of Northwestern
University and enrolled for the fall term. "The courses were
given in the evening," she wrote in the memoirs, "and did not
interfere with my administrative work." Credit was given for
the law readings with her father in Washington in 1882, and for
her courses in Zürich. Thus, with a year in the senior class at
Northwestern, she was able to graduate with a law degree in
June, 1894. By October of that year she was writing to Mrs.
Lloyd: "The law work goes well. I am trying our own prosecutions and attending lectures, and hope to be permitted to practice before the Supreme Court in July."

Although there is no record that she ever did appear before
the Court, her training and experience were permanent assets.
They provided her with the resources for such legal documents
as she might in the future choose to prepare. And they enabled
her to dramatize, for the layman, the havoc caused by successive
court decisions that for so many years systematically struck
down legislative efforts at reform.

A case in point was her scathing criticism of the Illinois
Supreme Court, which on March 15, 1895, declared unconstitutional the eight-hour clause (Section 5) of the Factory Act.[19]
The decision was a bitter blow, especially in light of the spirited
campaign preceding adoption of the bill, and the great sense of
accomplishment as the regulations began to take effect. As she
had written Engels on December 31, 1894:

> We have at last won a victory for our 8 hours law. The
> Supreme Court has handed down no decision sustaining it,

---

[18] *The Survey, op. cit.*, p. 274.
[19] *Ritchie* v. *The People*, 155 Ill. 98 (1895).

but the stockyards magnates having been arrested until they are tired of it, have instituted the 8 hours day for 10,000 employees, men, women and children. We have 18 suits pending to enforce the 8 hours law and we think we shall establish it permanently before Easter. It has been a painful struggle of eighteen months and the S C may annul the law. But I have strong hopes that the popular interest may prove too strong.

Now that the Supreme Court had acted as she had feared it might, she was impelled to make very clear just what that decision entailed. In her third Factory Inspector's Report she wrote:

This is not a question between the day of eight hours and the day of ten. In practice, the question is between an unlimited working day and a day restricted by statute to a reasonable maximum number of hours. . . . The effect of the decision has been the reestablishment of the unlimited working day for thousands of women and children in the factories and workshops of this State. Again, as before the enactment of the law, little girls just fourteen years of age may be employed twenty consecutive hours, as they actually are in establishments known to the inspectors.

Picking her way through a forest of citations, she pointed out that the Court had introduced "a new feature . . . into the body of American legal precedent" by identifying hiring for a given number of hours with the right of contract, and the right of contract with the right to property protected by the Fourteenth Amendment. The Court had thereby assumed that the regulation of hours was "not exclusively a matter of the Constitution of the State of Illinois," but of the Federal Constitution as well. By this reasoning, any curtailment of the working day was impossible. For while it might be easy to amend a State Constitution so as to include the power to regulate the length of the working day, "there is no prospect of any immediate change in the Constitution of the United States." But state regulation of hours, she argued, is constitutional; it has been proved so in both New York and Massachusetts, where such laws have been unequivocally upheld. Moreover:

When the observation of a few more years has convinced the medical profession, the philanthropists and the educators, as experience has already convinced the factory employees themselves, that it is a life and death matter to the young people who form so large a proportion of their number, to have a working day of reasonable length guaranteed by law, it will be found possible to rescue the Fourteenth Amendment to the Constitution of the United States from the perverted application upon which this decision rests. We may hope that Ritchie v. The People will then be added to the reversed decisions in which the Supreme Court of Illinois is so rich.[20]

Her hope was eventually fulfilled, but in the meantime the damage done by the Court extended even beyond the walls of factory and workshop. In ironic understatement, writing in the *New England Magazine* several years later, Florence Kelley commented:

> After the annulment of the eight-hours law by the Supreme Court of Illinois, in 1895, two of the best literature classes [at Hull House] were broken up because the girls who composed them were obliged to resume the practice (beneficently interrupted by the law) of working at the Electric Works until nine o'clock at night.[21]

[20] All quotations relative to the Supreme Court decision are from a section entitled "The Supreme Court Annuls the Eight-Hour Section," in *Illinois—Factory Inspector's Report*, 1895 (Springfield, Ill., 1896), pp. 5-7.

[21] "Hull House," in *New England Magazine*, Vol. XVIII, No. 5, July, 1898, p. 561.

CHAPTER XIII

The Inspector Moves Afield

Among the demands made on Florence Kelley, both in office and out, was one that she constantly made upon herself: to share as widely as possible her experiences in the field of reform in order to quicken the business of reform. It was "the writer's work of education" again, but now the writer was an active participant rather than just an observer. While she enjoyed teaching and lecturing for the direct personal contact involved, these activities were necessarily limited. To reach a larger audience, she must rely on her published articles and reports, and these she worked out with the greatest of care.

One has only to compare her Factory Inspector's Reports with those of her successor, to appreciate not only the comprehensive tables and graphs, but also the insights and constructive, analytical criticism that went into them. The inclusion of a scholarly critique of a State Supreme Court decision is but one illustration of what role she felt her reports should play. She regarded each one not as routine duty, but rather in the nature of a sociological study, to be broadly utilized and continually improved upon. "I am very desirous of making these reports valuable to students," she wrote Ely (August 22, 1895).

It was in the same educational light that she looked upon the Proceedings of the Factory Inspectors' annual conventions, to which she regularly contributed a paper. The custom was for the delegates, at the close of each convention, to order copies of the Proceedings for home consumption. In the midst of the usual orders for twenty-five or fifty, with a rare request for a hundred, the thousand copies ordered by Chief Inspector Kelley

for Illinois, at the Seventh Annual Convention,[1] created something of a stir. She made good use of them, too, distributing
them "generously . . . among [the state's] public men of every
character," as the Secretary took pains to note in his report
the following year.[2]

Other articles, too, were beginning to flow from her pen. One
jointly with Mrs. Stevens and another under her own signature had been prepared for publication in a German journal of
legislation and statistics. The plan was changed, however, when
she was asked by Ely to reserve them for a volume of studies on
the Chicago working class, one of a series in a "Library of
Economics and Politics" which he was editing for Thomas Y.
Crowell and Company. This volume, fifth in the series, was to
become the noted *Hull House Maps and Papers*.

The project was not without its irritations and frustrations.
As she wrote Ely on November 14, 1894:

> I sent today to Crowell & Co. the corrected proof of the
> two chapters on The Sweating System and Wage-Earning
> Children. . . .
> I am, of course, disappointed at the delay in getting out
> the book after I held back my essays from the Archiv fur
> soziale Gesetzgebung (which pays liberally and promptly),
> because you wrote me in May that the book would be in
> the market last Sept.
> But the disappointment over the delay is trivial in com-
> parison with the dismay which I felt when you suggested
> cutting the maps. This I positively decline to permit.
> The charts are mine to the extent that I not only fur-
> nished the data for them but hold the sole permission from
> the U.S. department of labor to publish them. I have never
> contemplated, and do not now contemplate, any form of
> publication except as two linen-backed maps or charts, fold-

---

[1] Held in Chicago, Sept. 19-22, 1893. In the absence of the Mayor, who was
"unavoidably detained with other important official engagements," Florence Kelley
"extended to the Convention a cordial welcome to the hospitality of the City and
State, with the hope that the occasion would prove one of great profit, as she felt
certain it would of much pleasure to all present." *International Association of Factory
Inspectors of North America*, Annual Conventions, 1893-1899, 7-13, pp. 4, 132.

[2] *Ibid.*, Eighth Annual Convention, p. 103. At this Convention, Florence Kelley
made and the delegates adopted a proposal that the status of all state laws governing
wages, hours, sweatshop and tenement house manufacture, safety and sanitation
inspection, and allied subjects, be made a part of the annual convention proceedings
(p. 26). A digest of such laws appeared in subsequent Proceedings for a number
of years.

ing in pockets in the cover of the book, similar to Mr. Booth's charts.[3]

If Crowell & Co. do not contemplate this, it will be well to stop work at once, as I can consent to no use of my charts in any other form.

She won her point, and the *Maps and Papers* appeared in 1895 in the format she had envisioned.

The vehemence is understandable. It was not just that she had contributed the first two of the book's eleven chapters, using much of the material in her Inspector's reports. The volume itself had come into being largely as a consequence of the slum investigation, of which she had been in charge. The two "maps or charts," color-keyed to show nationality and income respectively, were based on figures taken from the government schedules she had processed. She had always intended to make use of the data, and the proposal to publish the volume offered an opportunity that she was determined not to let slip.

Her tenacity was justified, for the book sold well; in two years the edition was exhausted. However, "The Boston publishers," Jane Addams remarked a bit wistfully, "did not consider it worthy of a second [printing]."[4] Yet the work still stands as an illumination of Chicago working-class life at the time, and a valuable source book for students of the early philosophy of social settlements.

While adhering to that philosophy in general—indeed, she spent the greater part of her life as a settlement resident— Florence Kelley's own attitude toward the role of the settlement house was later to undergo some modification. In an article written in 1906 from the Henry Street Settlement in New York where she was then living, she singled out what she considered a fundamental flaw: that slums were simply taken for granted as inevitable. "Everyone seems to have assumed overcrowding as permanent and to have set about dealing [only] with the

---

[3] Charles Booth, ed., *Labour and Life of the People* (London and Edinburgh, 1891), 2 vols. "Maps of London poverty" attached to cover of appendix. Republished in revised form as the first four volumes of the author's *Life and Labour of the People in London* (London and New York, 1892-97), 9 vols. Mrs. Kelley praises it as a "monumental work" in "My Novitiate," *The Survey*, Apr. 1, 1927, p. 34 and note.

[4] Addams, *op. cit.*, p. 153.

results."[5] She herself, she confessed, had also followed "this line of action and thoughtlessness." At the same time, it was the part of her own disposition and training to "set about dealing with" causes, even as she sought to cope with results. And perhaps her choice of residence symbolized for her the necessity to combine both courses.

It would have been out of character for Florence Kelley, while conscientiously fulfilling the claims of her office, to have confined her activities to them alone. Thus it was that shortly after the crisis of the smallpox epidemic, she became personally involved in a labor-capital conflict of national import. The occasion was the struggle of the railwaymen in the depression spring of 1894.

Made desperate by a series of wage cuts, workers on the Great Northern Railroad, members of the American Railway Union under Eugene Debs, had struck against the line and won. The victory emboldened the men at the Pullman Car works who had just been notified of a twenty-five percent wage cut, and on May 11 three thousand, many of them also members of the ARU, walked off the job in protest. The June convention of the Union voted support, and (against Debs' advice) a boycott on hauling Pullman cars. Arbitration failed, and the strike began on June 28. Four days later the company obtained a blanket injunction under the Sherman Anti-Trust Act. But now there could be no turning back, nor would Debs have attempted any. On July 10 he and three others were indicted for conspiracy (to obstruct a mail train on the Rock Island Railroad). Released the next day on bail, they were jailed again a week later on charges of contempt of court for violating the injunction.[6]

The arrests and the outrageous nature of the injunction brought Florence Kelley at once into the fray. On July 18 she wrote Lloyd:

Debs is in jail and his courage, while not failing needs all the bracing it can get. And the length of his imprisonment

---

[5] "The Settlements: Their Lost Opportunity," in *Charities and the Commons* (later *The Survey*), Apr. 7, 1906, pp. 79-81. Her point here was that the settlements should have taken the lead in efforts for more and better housing and to halt the developing slums.

[6] Ray Ginger, *The Bending Cross* (Rutgers University Press, 1949), pp. 100-151, *passim*. Actually, Debs had issued orders that all mail trains be moved. *Ibid.*, p. 123.

Eugene V. Debs

Clarence Darrow

may, perhaps, be modified by the degree of public interest shown in the present injunction outrage. Fancy an injunction that makes it a crime "to *attempt to induce by persuasion* any person to refrain from handling a *freight* car"! Yet I read this injunction containing these words, posted in the Rock Island yards. (*Her emphasis.*)

So I am trying to arrange a Central Music Hall meeting and Darrow will speak and, I hope, Bemis and Zeublin and Dr. Holmes. I do not know yet who else. It is a national calamity that you are away from Chicago now when the public mind is seething and the time is ripe for such far-reaching action. . . .

Can you write a letter to the meeting? The date is not fixed, but the fact that there will be such a meeting is certainly determined. Probably next Thursday week.

It will be a meeting of citizens of Chicago to protest against government by injunction and rifles.

Not too many of her fellow citizens, however, were ready to share her sense of urgency. In a letter to Lloyd a fortnight later she recited her difficulties. An attempt to secure bail from a "respectable businessman" was unsuccessful. "Frank E. Brown, cashier of the First National Bank . . . indignantly repudiated the idea of associating his name in any way with the strike or strikers." A number of others were equally unresponsive, so that "when the time came for giving bail, this was done by those arch publicans and sinners William Skakel and William Fitzgerald." She had also written to some possible sponsors of the protest meeting: "Bayard Holmes, Zeublin, Bemis, Dr. Hirsch, Mrs. Henrotin, Mrs. Wilmarth, Mrs. Kean, Miss Willard, Mrs. Harvey." Again the response was indifferent, although "Mrs. Kean sent five dollars and a glowing letter of sympathy and encouragement." Clarence Darrow was enthusiastic about the plan for such a meeting, and at first agreed to "make a speech and pay twenty-five dollars towards the cost. But he has since undertaken a very valuable part of the work of the legal defense of the Debs men and justly withdraws from the stage defense." Finally, both Central Music Hall and the Auditorium were under repair, "and cannot be had for any price before September 1st."[7]

Although she makes no further reference to the meeting (the

---

[7] FK to HDL, Aug. 1, 1894.

project seems finally to have been dropped), her interest in Debs and his cause did not waver. That she found so little support in the liberal community at the time is perhaps not surprising, in view of the violent press campaign that continued well after Federal intervention had broken the strike. But a year later, when the legal maneuvers that sent Debs and the ARU leaders back to jail—not for conspiracy but only for contempt—could be looked at in a saner light, she scored a gratifying success. With Lloyd and Judge Lyman Trumbull she organized a huge reception for Debs on his release from Woodstock Prison on November 22, 1895. The Chicago Trades and Labor Assembly sponsored it, Lloyd and Governor Davis H. Waite of Colorado spoke in welcome, and the old Battery D Armory "was filled to the walls with standing men and women" in delirious acclaim.[8]

Along with the continual enrichment of outlook through these and other experiences, Florence Kelley was also beginning to reach some definite opinions on what an American brand of socialism should be. For party activity as such she seems to have had neither time nor inclination. But the substance of her work was so closely identified with the subject matter of socialist theory that her inevitable concern was how best to utilize that theory for social change through social action.

In her early days in Chicago she had spoken freely wherever and whenever the opportunity arose, and her appointment as Chief Factory Inspector did not limit her. "As Governor Altgeld places no restriction whatever upon our freedom of speech," she had written Engels (November 21, 1893), "and the English etiquette of silence while in the civil service is unknown here, we are not hampered by our position, and three of my deputies and my assistant are outspoken socialists and active in agitation."

The problem was how to enlarge the little band of the enlightened. In Lloyd she had quickly recognized a kindred spirit —an explorer of the same questions that had troubled her, a man closely tied to labor, who associated himself with "the

---

[8] Ginger, *op. cit.*, pp. 175, 177. Trumbull, former member of the Illinois Supreme Court, had served a term as U. S. Senator. During the summer of 1894 he campaigned for the Populists.

principle of the collective ownership and control of all the means of production."[9] This was the kind of person, she thought, that America needed, not only as a man of letters but in the political field as well. In the summer of 1894 she had urged him to run for Congress from the Seventh District on the Labor-Populist ticket,[10] and was delighted when he accepted the nomination. When his *Wealth Against Commonwealth* appeared that September, she greeted it as a significant breakthrough in American economic thought. Writing to Mrs. Lloyd on the last day of October, she expressed her appreciation in glowing terms:

> After my night school is over, I read Wealth vs. Commonwealth, and rejoice that the first of the great American contributions to economics is made, and the way paved for a literature. I think Mr. Lloyd's campaign is the beginning of the new era in our national life.
>
> This is not wild personal enthusiasm. It is my honest conviction that it lies in the power of a few enlightened persons to use these last six years of our century for the work of peaceful transition. And the greatest contribution that one man can make, is to show what the disorder is and then take his part in changing that disorder by means of the machinery already at hand. I envy Mr. Lloyd his opportunity and his equipment for its use. Both seem to me the noblest that have fallen to any man's lot since the days of struggle from 1850 to 1865. I hope and believe that his strength will increase now that the book is off his mind.

Lloyd himself had at first felt that he could be more effective out of office, and had only reluctantly consented to run. But he did consider the People's Party "a useful vehicle for expressing popular grievances."[11] In that Party's first national campaign in 1892, their presidential ticket of Generals James B. Weaver and James G. Field had polled more than a million votes out of a total of 12,000,000, on a platform that included free silver, government ownership of the railroads and telegraph system, land and financial reforms, direct election of the President, Vice-President and Senators, and adoption of the

---

[9] Destler, *op. cit.*, p. 264.

[10] Lloyd was in Little Compton, R. I., when she wired him (Aug. 13): "Please do not decline nomination in the 7 Congressional District no one else can do so much good at this time." Lloyd answered (Aug. 15): "...I should consider it a sacred duty to serve if elected. But I can not make a canvass." Nor would he run under rumored Democratic endorsement. Letter in possession of Kelley family.

[11] Destler, *op. cit.*, p. 274.

Australian ballot.[12] Since then Lloyd, who had held aloof from that campaign, had begun working to draw the Populist program further in the direction of socialization and antimonopolism. At the Springfield convention of Populists and trades unionists in May, 1894, and again at the Illinois Federation of Labor's Industrial Conference in the same city in July, he had taken a leading part in drafting the statements of principles and platforms. These combined the most progressive features of Populist and labor programs with his own ideas on a welfare democracy, and became the basis for an Illinois Labor-Populist coalition.[13]

During the next two years Lloyd was at the heart of the struggle waged by the labor and socialist forces to hold the coalition together against repeated attempts by the silverites to replace the Labor-Populist program with a single free-silver plank. But it was a losing battle. His prediction that the national Populist leaders would eventually hand over their party to the free-silverites had its first confirmation when the Populists scheduled their 1896 nominating convention to take place after that of the Democratic Party.[14] The reason offered for this move was that both major parties would nominate "Wall Street" candidates; whereupon the Populists, having hoisted the alluring flag of free silver, would gather bolting dissidents from both camps into their own.

Faced with this situation, Lloyd was uncertain about attending the convention at all. Particularly distasteful was the fact that the Illinois delegation he was to head would be under challenge from a rival Cook County free silver group. Could anything worthwhile be salvaged from the impending wreck of the populist ideal? He talked the question over at length with Florence Kelley one June evening before the round of conventions had begun.

Her interest was immediately aroused. Earlier that year she

---

[12] John D. Hicks, *The Populist Revolt* (University of Nebraska Press, 1961), p. 210. (Originally published U. of Minn. Press, 1931.)

[13] Destler, *op. cit.*, pp. 267-70, 277-79. Destler describes the Labor-Populist coalition as "the progressive unions, ARU, a few Fabians, radical Single-Taxers, gradualist Socialists, and a handful of orthodox urban Populists" (p. 277).

[14] The Republican National Convention was held in St. Louis June 22; the Democratic Convention in Chicago July 7; the Populist Convention in St. Louis July 22.

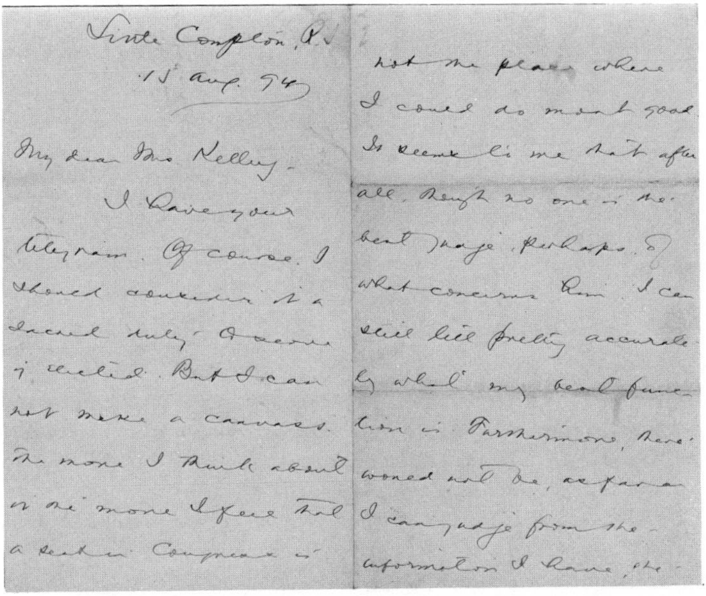

Facsimile, Henry Demarest Lloyd to Florence Kelley

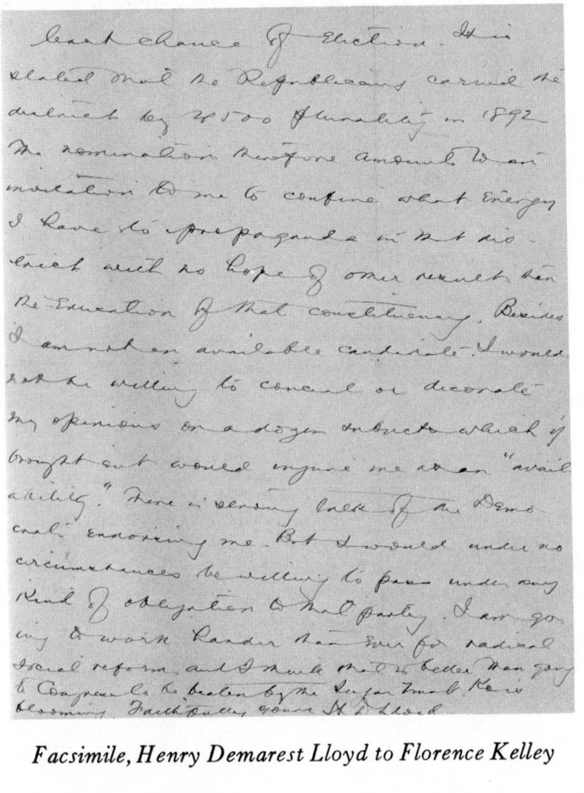

Little Compton, R. I.

15 Aug. 94

My dear Mrs. Kelley—

I have your telegram. Of course, I should consider it a sacred duty to serve if elected. But I cannot make a canvass. The more I think about it the more I feel that a seat in Congress is not the place where I could do most good. It seems to me that after all, though no one is the best judge, perhaps, of what concerns him, I can still tell pretty accurately what my best function is. Furthermore, there would not be, as far as I can judge from the information I have, the least chance of election. It is stated that the Republicans carried the district by 4500 plurality in 1892. The nomination therefore amounts to an invitation to me to confine what energy I have to propaganda in that district with no hope of other result than the education of that constituency. Besides I am not an available candidate. I would not be willing to conceal or decorate my opinions on a dozen subjects which if brought out would injure me as an "availability." There is serious talk of the Democrats endorsing me. But I would under no circumstances be willing to pass under any kind of obligation to that party. I am going to work harder than ever for radical social reform and I think that is better than going to Congress to be beaten by the Sugar Trust. Ko is blooming.

Faithfully yours,

H. D. Lloyd

Text of letter, H. D. Lloyd to F. Kelley

had been too engrossed with the necessities of office to give much attention to the problems of politics. A strike of garment workers, and refusal of the manufacturers to arbitrate, had left thousands of men, women and children unemployed, "with nothing laid by" to tide them over. In March, she had asked Lloyd to write the resolutions for a mass meeting to "protest against the sweating system" and to rally support for the strikers.[15] Now as she listened to him her mind busied itself with the political complement to the economic problems that were her especial province.

The conversation that evening reached no conclusions, but she took the question home with her. By the following day (June 18) she had put her thoughts enough in order to write them out for Lloyd:

> I have been thinking over the question which you asked me last evening, in regard to the convention at St. Louis. I have not given the subject any previous attention, and was not prepared to reply out of hand. What I do think is this: that the present Socialist organization in this country is a most undesirable one. The practice of expelling every-one who can speak English from the Socialist Labor Party, while not literally followed, is so nearly universal, that the party is very largely a bunch of greenhorns. If there could be segregated from the Populist party a body, however small, of Socialists of American nationality and traditions, this seems to me worth a very great sacrifice indeed.
>
> Such a body could win followers. This the Socialist Labor Party under its present leadership, and following of its present policy, can never do. I hold to the whole platform of the Socialist Party. But it had not occurred to me, until after my conversation with you last evening, that this *may* be the opportunity to obtain a nucleus of Americans to adopt that platform, yet who would never, of their own accord, enter the Socialist Labor Party as at present con-stituted. I am such an American. I could never affiliate with any party which made Silver the burden of its cry. But I cannot stand the scurrility of the People, the organ of the Socialist Labor Party. Nor do I approve of the policy of splitting trades unions which is one of the favorite activities of the present leaders of the S.L.P. But I would make a good deal of sacrifice for the sake of working with a party of American Socialists.

---

[15] FK to HDL, Mar. 3, 1896.

It does not seem to me at present, as though anything less than an attempt at getting the remnant of the Populists to undertake such a movement, were worth taking the trouble about.

Thus, from the tangled web of Populist politics, Florence Kelley hoped to extricate the practical means for achieving the goal toward which theory had been urging her ever since her adventures with the New York SLP. The need for a party which would be socialist in principles, American in appeal, had so often been the subject of her exchanges with Engels. Now, Engels had been dead for almost a year; and for the first time there seemed to be at hand a little body of like-minded individuals, "of American nationality and traditions," ready to move in a radical direction. It was perhaps an earnest of her deep emotional as well as intellectual involvement that she used the word "sacrifice" twice in her letter to Lloyd.

That such a crystallization failed to take place at the time was more a judgment on the period than on the goal. Indeed, something akin to her notion did emerge in 1901 with the founding of the Socialist Party of Debs, although by then she was too absorbed in her new national duties to take immediate part.[16]

We have no answer of Lloyd's to the June letter, but whatever he may have thought of her critical comment, he did go to the convention—and sat in agonized silence through all the sessions. Denied the floor, deserted by allies he had counted on, he watched the Populists enter "that bourne from which no reform party returns." After the delegates had vociferously accepted the Democratic nominee Bryan as their own, Lloyd left the hall and, for a long time, all politics.[17]

Understanding his disgust and despair, FlorenceKelley nonetheless tried to draw him back and into the gubernatorial campaign that fall.

---

[16] A decade later she was one of a group that founded the Intercollegiate Socialist Society, which she served variously as executive committee member, vice-president and president; when the name was changed to League for Industrial Democracy she served two more years (1921-23) as vice-president. Harry W. Laidler recalls that in 1912, much moved by a speech on child labor by Debs during the election campaign, she enrolled in the Socialist Party, and retained membership for several years. Interview with Dr. Laidler, Feb. 6, 1959.

[17] Destler, *op. cit.*, pp. 286-87.

We miss you very much in the campaign (*she wrote October* 1). Things are badly muddled, and Governor Altgeld's friends seem few, indeed, in this time of need. The Socialists and labor skates are knifing him alike. The silver populists and the straight trades-union vote seem to be his main hope besides the farmers. And if the working people allow him to be defeated now, in the face of his record, surely they deserve to have no other friend until this generation dies out and another and better one takes its place. . . .

I don't know whether you want Governor Altgeld re-elected—everything is so confused this year that I don't feel certain of much in any direction! But if you do—he needs every bit of help, of every kind, that every friend can give him until election day.

Her plea had some effect. Lloyd wrote to a number of friends among the Illinois reformers, that it would be a "great misfortune" if Altgeld were defeated. But beyond that, and a letter to the *New York Journal* in defense of Altgeld, he took no part.[18]

Under no illusions herself, Florence Kelley saw only too clearly the steady erosion of Altgeld support. On October 15 she wrote Lloyd ruefully: "I think the State is lost." It was indeed. Three weeks later Altgeld went down to defeat as the Republicans swept every major (and almost every minor) office in Illinois.

---

[18] The *Journal* letter answered an attack against Altgeld by Theodore Roosevelt, then Police Commissioner of New York. Destler, *op. cit.*, p. 288.

CHAPTER XIV

The Role Confirmed

It had long been a custom in Illinois for the outgoing governor to deliver his farewell address at the inauguration ceremony of his successor. When the newly elected John R. Tanner refused Altgeld this courtesy,[1] his action merely foreshadowed others of similar political callousness and spite.

One such was his abrupt dismissal in August, 1897, of the Chief Factory Inspector and her entire staff. There had been no previous intimation. Over the spring and summer Florence Kelley had worked as usual. In preparation for the Eleventh Annual Convention of the International Association of Factory Inspectors, to be held in Detroit beginning August 31, she had written a paper, "Evolution of the Illinois Child Labor Law," which cited the gains in labor and protective legislation since the establishment of her office. The Saturday before the convention was to open, she was notified that her appointment had been cancelled.

The brief note with which she dispatched her paper to Rufus R. Wade, president of the I.A.F.I., made no attempt to conceal her feelings:

> Dear Sir—Enclosed please find a paper in which I have tried to combine a statement of our progress in legislation since the last convention, with the substance of the paper I had promised for the year.
>
> I prepared it with the full expectation of attending the convention, and am denied that pleasure by my unforeseen removal August 28th.
>
> I shall be greatly obliged if you will have the secretary

[1] Waldo R. Browne, *Altgeld of Illinois* (New York, 1924), p. 298.

read it at the convention, as this will be the only paper from Illinois this year.[2]

The crassness of her dismissal was compounded by the character of the man selected to replace her. Louis Arrington had been on the payroll for twenty-seven years at the Alton works of the Illinois Glass Company—an institution notorious for its employment of several hundred boys whose ages ranged downward to seven and eight, and who were generally kept at work until three in morning. Moreover, he had been convicted of violating the very act he was now appointed to enforce. No wonder that, as Florence Kelley wrote later, "Throughout his term of office there were no prosecutions for violations of law by glass manufacturers, nor was the child labor law of Illinois amended."[3]

In addition to being severed from work to which she had given her whole heart, Florence Kelley once again faced the difficulty of providing for her family. With her regular income terminated, she must put together enough odds and ends to keep going.

One source of revenue was found in the articles she published in the *Archiv für soziale Gesetzgebung und Statistik*, for which she served as American Editor, 1897-1898. Several years earlier she had already had a paper accepted, "Factory Legislation in the United States." Then in 1897 "Women as Factory Inspectors in the United States," appeared, and three more contributions were printed the following year.[4]

More dependable was an evening job she obtained in Novem-

[2] *International Association of Factory Inspectors, op. cit.*, Eleventh Annual Convention, p. 33. The paper was read by Mrs. F. S. Greene, of Chicago, "with interpolations by herself."

[3] Destler, *op. cit.*, p. 427; Florence Kelley, *Some Ethical Gains Through Legislation*, p. 57; a lengthy description of conditions in the glass works is found in her Factory Inspector's Report for 1895, pp. 14-18.

[4] "Die Fabrikgesetzgebung der Vereinigten Staaten," in *Archiv*, etc., No. 8, 1895, pp. 192-209. (It is interesting that Sorge refers to this article and gives a brief resume in *Die Neue Zeit*, 1895-96, pp. 537-38.) "Die weibliche Fabrikinspektion in den Vereinigten Staaten," in *Archiv*, etc., No. 11, 1897, pp. 127-42. *Ibid.*, No. 12, 1898: "Das Sweating system in den Vereinigten Staaten," pp. 208-32; "Die gesetzliche Regelung der Kinderarbeit im Staate Illinois," pp. 530-50; "Drei Entscheidungen Oberster Gerichte über den gesetzlichen Arbeitstag in den Vereinigten Staaten," pp. 744-74. She contributed eight articles in all to the *Archiv*, the last appearing in 1901.

ber, 1897, at the John Crerar Library.[5] The pay was slender—
fifty dollars a month—and her duties as assistant to the periodical clerk in no wise exhausted all her talents. But it was
security of a sort, and in an institution devoted to science, tech-
nology and medicine there was much to satisfy her interests.
After her evening's work she would return to the living room at
Hull House, and over a cup of hot chocolate recount with wit
and sparkle her experiences with patrons of the library.[6]

Her days now freed from the labors of factory inspection,
Florence Kelley found herself increasingly in demand as a
speaker.[7] Effective as she was with her pen, she was at her very
best before an audience. Using no notes, or only the barest
jotted guide, she spoke with a "beautiful and precise use of
words," and a remarkable control of her voice. Her manner was
direct and unadorned, but the very simplicity of her delivery
added to the drama of her subject matter. "I only heard her
speak once," a young woman said, "but she changed the whole
course of my life."[8]

Most of these speeches went unrecorded, but those which
were delivered as papers at various conventions appear in the
proceedings and are available for study. One of Florence Kelley's greatest assets, as she had demonstrated a decade earlier
when she spoke to the New York Association of Collegiate
Alumnae, was the ability to present the subject of her own
interest in terms that would engage the concern of those she
addressed. Rapport thus established, she drove home her points,
and her favored topics were constantly embellished and given
new aspects through interaction with an ever-changing audience. It was the same with her articles, whether she wrote for
the specialized journals, the women's magazines or publications
of general interest. The first paragraph or so would contain

---

[5] Mrs. Kelley held the library post from Nov. 8, 1897, to April 30, 1899. Letter
from Herman H. Hinkle, Librarian, July 12, 1963. In September, 1898, her salary
was raised to $60.00 a month. FK to CBK, Sept. 21, 1898.

[6] Alice Hamilton, *Exploring the Dangerous Trades* (Boston, 1943), p. 62.

[7] Goldmark, *op. cit.*, p. 47.

[8] Interview with Mr. Nicholas Kelley, Mar. 9, 1959. A diligent analysis of Mrs.
Kelley's speaking style may be found in Ramona Tomlin Mattson, *A Critical Evaluation of Florence Kelley's Speaking on the Child Labor Issue,* unpublished doctoral
dissertation, University of Iowa. (University Microfilm, Ann Arbor, Mich., 1956.)
344-45.

the precise idea to strike an answering spark from the readers she sought to reach.

Throughout her tenure as Chief Factory Inspector, her annual reports and her papers at the Annual Conventions, while discussing the routine problems of factory inspection, presented those problems in a far from routine fashion. Pity and anger set aflame the impersonal graphs and tables; the figures were never impersonal to her. "It is boys and girls," she wrote in later years, "and not percentages that are maimed."[9]

As a delegate to the Twenty-third National Convention of the Conference of Charities and Correction in 1896, she had discussed "The Working Child" from the standpoint of the problem he presented to correctional institutions. Far from building moral stamina, she said, sending children to work at an early age—as cash girls and boys, as messenger and telegraph boys—subjects them to temptations they have not yet learned to resist. They gain neither education nor skill on these jobs, and are useless and burnt out by the time they might have qualified as adult labor. "The only way to deal effectively with the child labor problem," she declared, "is to keep all the children in school, to turn all working children into school children."[10]

Later that year, discussing vocational training in the *American Journal of Sociology*, she proposed trade schools for children, but of a kind new for her day—and still pertinent for ours. Writing on "The Working Boy,"[11] she asked the question: How do we educate for this "epoch of industrial instability" which increasing specialization has created? Do we permit the narrowing of the job to be reflected in a narrowing of training? Should we not rather "insist on the education of all the thinking powers of all the workers?" The future of the nation depends on its children, and the future of the children largely depends on their schools. "Instead of working all head and no hands in the primary schools, and all hands and no head forever after in some brainless wretched manipulation, let us have every child

---

[9] "The Manufacturers' Program Won't Do," in *The Survey*, June 15, 1928, pp. 344-45.

[10] *Conference of Charities and Correction* (Boston and London, 1896), Vol. 23, p. 162. (23rd National Convention, June 4-10, 1896.)

[11] *American Journal of Sociology*, Nov. 1896, pp. 358-68.

using both head and hands in every grade from kindergarten to high school."

Invited in the spring of 1898 to contribute a paper to the hearings being held by the Senate and House on the suffrage question, she took as her subject "The Need of the Ballot for Women as Industrial Factors." Votelessness, she pointed out, places women on a "level of irresponsibility." As one fifth of the labor force in manufacturing and commerce, women must have some sort of legislative voice in controlling their working conditions. They are accused of lowering wages when they enter the labor market; too often that is the only way they can get into the market at all. Even so, she emphasized, the matter of suffrage must not be approached from the single point of view of "actual money wages," but of the wider needs of "woman as a human being and a member of the community."[12]

When Florence Kelley had first begun, in 1888, to gather data on the problem of the working child, she may have been interested solely in producing a statistical study. But as she proceeded, the study was transformed from an end in itself into a means for exploring ways to cure the evil of child labor. That evil, as she pointed out, had many roots, so that any cure must be equally diversified. To such scattered prohibitory legislation and compulsory school laws as already existed, she had proposed adding a third force, that of the buying public.

The idea was first implemented when the New York Consumers' League came into being in January, 1891. For several years this league remained the only such group; none, for example, existed in Chicago when Florence Kelley first arrived there. But in December, 1893, six months after her appointment as Chief Factory Inspector, she was invited by the Chicago

---

[12] The National American Woman Suffrage Association was holding its 30th Annual Convention in Washington, D.C., at this time, Feb. 13-19, 1898. The Congressional hearings were on Tuesday, Feb. 15. The House of Representatives Judiciary Committee considered "the practical workings of suffrage wherever it is exercised by women." The Senate Special Committee on Woman Suffrage directed its attention to "the philosophy of the movement." Mrs. Kelley's paper (read by Mary A. Swift of California) was presented to the Senate Committee. *Minutes, National American Woman Suffrage Association,* 1898, pp. 18-20; Elizabeth Cady Stanton, Susan B. Anthony, Mathilda Jocelyn Gage, *The History of Woman Suffrage* (Rochester, 1881-1902), IV, 311-13. Here the title of Mrs. Kelley's paper appears as "The Working Woman's Need of the Ballot."

Branch of the Association of Collegiate Alumnae to speak on "The Formation of a Purchasers' League to Protect Women and Children." At that meeting a committee of three was appointed by the Branch to "confer with other committees" about the possibility of forming such a league in Chicago.

Very little seems to have been done beyond conferring until several years later, when Dr. John Graham Brooks, who had been active in consumers' affairs in Boston, came to Chicago to deliver a course of lectures on Industrial Conditions. A number of women, including members of the Association of Collegiate Alumnae, attended the lectures and were moved to act. In February, 1897, a Consumers' League of Chicago was informally organized under the auspices of the Association, of which Mrs. Kenneth R. Smoot was chairman. At that meeting Mrs. Smoot set up a committee to begin visiting shops and to lay the groundwork for a permanent organization. In November a circular was issued, addressed to the Women's Clubs of Chicago. Headed "Recommendations for Shopping," it asked women shoppers to adhere to certain self-imposed regulations in order to make the holiday season easier for department store workers. Two weeks before Christmas one of the Association members took a job as a saleswoman so as to get first-hand information on behind-the-counter conditions. By December 18 a provisional constitution had been prepared for membership approval.[13]

By this time the Consumers' League movement had begun to grow in other areas. With the help of the New York City organization under Mrs. Maud Nathan, Brooklyn and Philadelphia had each set up a league in 1896, Syracuse two years later. In Boston the first formal steps toward organization were taken in March, 1897, at a meeting called by Dr. Brooks and addressed by Mrs. Nathan; the establishment of a Massachusetts Consumers' League was voted the following June.

During the Boston discussions, a committee had been appointed to study the idea of a Consumers' Label to be awarded

---

[13] Talbot and Rosenberry, op. cit., p. 109; Mrs. Charles Russell Lowell, "Consumers' Leagues," in Church Social Union, Feb. 15, 1898, pp. 22-23; Annie Marion MacLean, "Two Weeks in Department Stores," in American Journal of Sociology, Vol. 4, July, 1898-May, 1899, pp. 721-41. Florence Kelley included a translation of the "Recommendations for Shopping" in her Archiv article on the regulation of child labor in Illinois.

Maud Nathan, president of the New York Consumers League

No. 1

No. 2

No. 3

No 4

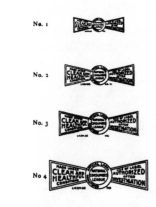

NATIONAL CONSUMERS' LEAGUE

105 East 22d Street, New York City

November, 1906

Goods bearing this label are made in factories in which—

1. The State Factory Law is obeyed
2. ALL the goods are made on premises approved by the League
3. Overtime is not worked
4. Children under sixteen years of age are not employed

This guaranty is based upon the following procedure: Before the use of the label is awarded to a manufacturer his factory is visited by an agent of the League, who also asks both the local Board of Health and the State Factory Inspector for a special report on the establishment. When this is satisfactory the manufacturer signs a penalty contract embodying the four points guaranteed. After the use of the label is awarded, the factory is visited from time to time by the agent of the League, and the local committee of the League reports upon it to the National Secretary

Please destroy all previous lists

Back and front pages of a National Consumers League pamphlet, showing various sizes of the Consumers' Label for approved "White Goods", and conditions under which it was awarded

to manufacturers who met the fair labor specifications laid down by the League. To this end it was proposed to investigate the working conditions of the Boston manufacturers of "white goods and cloaks" and to urge leading dry goods firms to stock goods made under fair conditions. Since many retailers were outlets for New York manufacturers, it was thought advisable to look into the latter too. W. L. Mackenzie King—later to become Prime Minister of Canada—was hired to investigate the Boston retail shops, at the rate of "$3.00 for four hours work"; and in October one of the League members "was asked to inquire whether the services of Mrs. Florence Kelley as inspector [of the New York firms] could be secured, if desired."[14]

Florence Kelley may have declined the offer, or it may not have been made at all; at any rate, someone else was eventually retained for the work. Several months later, however, (February, 1898) she wrote to the Massachusetts League, setting forth her ideas on a Consumers' Label and on its relation to the union label. This letter does not appear in the League files, but the Massachusetts minutes indicate that it touched off a lively discussion among the members.

Her letter may also have gone out to the other leagues; it certainly reached the chairman of the New York organization. In March Mrs. Nathan wrote to Boston enclosing a copy of a letter she had sent in reply. Although Mrs. Nathan's letter too is missing, its general content can be reconstructed from the discussion it evoked. The minutes of the meeting record that an agreement was finally reached to "further the interests of the trades-union label," without, however, making it "a requisite of the Consumers' League label."[15]

The sort of problem raised by the debate over the label certainly added to the rapidly growing conviction that a national organization was needed. Accordingly, within a few weeks a call for a conference of local leagues went out from the Con-

---

[14] *Minutes*, Massachusetts Consumers' League: March, May, June 7, Sept. 23, Oct. 7, Oct. 21, 1897. Typewritten copy in NCL files, Box 5-A, Library of Congress. Original in the Women's Archives, Radcliffe College.

[15] *Minutes*, Massachusetts Consumers' League, *op. cit.*, March, 1898. See also Maud Nathan's "The Consumers' Label," in *North American Review*, February, 1898, pp. 250-54.

sumers' League of the City of New York. On Monday, May 16, at 10:30 A.M., delegates from the six leagues assembled in Calvary Parish House at 106 East 22nd Street, for two days of deliberations.[16]

To Florence Kelley this was a welcome development indeed. As representative of the Illinois Consumers' League she quickly assumed a leading role. Appointed to the committee to discuss the consumers' label, she spoke persuasively in favor of it, and finally moved that it be officially adopted. The vote was four to two, New York City, Illinois, Syracuse and Massachusetts for the label, Brooklyn and Pennsylvania against. The following day, May 17, the report was approved by the conference, and a committee of three, Mrs. Nathan, Katherine Coman of Boston and Florence Kelley, was named to work out the details. Mrs. Nathan, chairman of the committee, was to report on the form of the label, Miss Coman to look into the possibility of contracts with manufacturers, and Florence Kelley to "investigate the work and expense necessary to introduce the label."[17] Before they adjourned, the delegates adopted a provisional constitution to be submitted, along with the label committee report, to the individual leagues. For the moment, the new organization took the name of National Federation of Consumers Leagues.

That evening a mass meeting was held in Assembly Hall, at 156 Fifth Avenue. The speakers were introduced by Mrs. Nathan "with appropriate and witty remarks." Following the presidents of the Pennsylvania and Massachusetts Leagues, Florence Kelley took the rostrum. The large audience listened attentively as she described her experiences with the sweatshops of Chicago and the long struggle to clean them out. In particular she referred to the recent improvement in conditions in the cigar manufacturing shops there, and cited the young Illinois

[16] *New York City Consumers' League, Annual Reports,* 1892-1904, Report for the year ending December, 1898, p. 18. (The Massachusetts *Minutes* say "Albany Parish House," but also record a vote of thanks to Dr. Parks for the use of Calvary Rectory.)

[17] *Minutes,* Massachusetts Consumers' League, May 24, 1898. For assistance in locating much of the material on the formation of the National Consumers League, I am greatly indebted to Mr. Louis L. Athey, who is preparing a doctoral dissertation on Consumers' Leagues for the University of Delaware.

Consumers' League as an effective force in bringing about such a change.[18]

Having thus left a signal imprint on both conference and mass meeting, Florence Kelley went back to Chicago. She brought with her the provisional constitution and the label report, and, we may presume, an infectious enthusiasm for the new federation. The local League was still functioning as an informal body, and it was not until November 30, 1898, at a meeting held in Hull House, that the Illinois Consumers' League was formally organized and the national constitution ratified. Mrs. Charles Henrotin was elected president, and Florence Kelley was named as one of the two Hull House representatives to the League.[19]

Apart from her Consumers' League activities and her continued interest in protective legislation, the record makes only a few references to what Florence Kelley was thinking, as well as doing, through the greater part of 1898. One of these is in a letter to Lloyd, dated September 26, upon receiving a copy of his newest book, *Labor Copartnership*. After the Populist debacle, Lloyd had turned his energies toward an investigation of the cooperative movement, and his book was the product of travels that had taken him to England, Ireland and Holland.[20] She read the work with her customary thoroughness, and to her thanks added some commentary of her own:

> I think it must prove a very valuable contribution, indeed, to the labor movements in these days of positive effort. I have recently read, with a good deal of care, the Webb's criticism of the movement: and so far as I can see, they are quite right in saying that labor copartnership is not, in itself, socialism; but since it never claimed to be socialism, and does not wish to be socialism, I cannot see what that has to do with the matter, unless some Fabians may have been claiming that it was socialism without knowing it, as Sidney Webb, himself, once claimed that peddlers' licenses were preliminary symptoms of socialism!

18 *New York Times*, May 18, 1898. The two local League presidents were Anna Watmough, Pennsylvania, and Edith Howes, Massachusetts. Other speakers were Professor E. R. A. Seligman of Columbia University, and Colonel George E. Waring, former Street Cleaning Commissioner. A preliminary announcement of the meeting appeared in the *Times* on May 15.

19 MacLean, *op. cit.*, p. 22n; Florence Kelley, "Hull House," *New England Magazine*, *op. cit.*, p. 254.

20 Destler, *op. cit.*, pp. 380-89.

> There is no doubt in my mind, that this is the best field for the education of the mass of the people for self-government in industry; but it is a little discouraging that, here in America, we are not even entering upon this primary school.

While not participating in the movement herself, she was quick to appreciate anything that would seem to move the social order a bit nearer correction of its inequities. And it was typical that she should base her approval of cooperatives as much on their educative as on their economic value. Information and experience, she always felt, were the twin necessities to bring about the "enlightenment" required for any viable society. Indeed, it hurt her to see any occasion wasted, through indifference or ineptitude, for adding to the reserves of knowledge.

Something of this distress shows up in a letter she wrote to Ely near the end of the year, when she heard that he was planning to dispose of his economics papers. She had pressed the Crerar Library to take over the collection, but was told that "the present formative state of the library" made any purchases of unbound collections impossible.

> I was very sorry indeed (*she wrote on November* 12) to learn that this is [the] policy not only because it leads to the loss of the opportunity to acquire your collection, but because it shuts off the outlook for a long time to come, for acquiring the best sources of information on all the municipal questions which Chicago students and clubs are eagerly inquiring into. . . .
>
> I'm sorry that you are thinking of parting with the collection, for I do not believe that any one goes on collecting as efficiently as the original collector, in any subject; but since you wish to do so, I can only wish you success, and hope that the University of Chicago may prove wiser than our endowment. For I hope that the collection may come to Chicago where we are poor in all the equipment for economic research except the keen interest which is, perhaps, the most important item after all.

Although no hint of restlessness creeps into these few letters, there is little doubt that Florence Kelley missed both the exactions and the rewards of her former office. She could always keep herself busy enough; but the absence of a base from which to work left a void which no amount of writing and lecturing could fill. She was therefore overjoyed when, early in January, 1899, Dr. Brooks made a second visit to Chicago, this time to ask if she would consider becoming executive officer of the national consumers league movement.

"How happy a day it seemed to me when it occurred," she recalled many years later, "and how indescribably precious a day it seems to me now that I look back upon it after six-and-twenty years, when Mr. Brooks came to Hull House at a time when I had ceased to be Factory Inspector of Illinois and was striving to write out my reminiscences of that brief term." The responsibilities associated with the offer, she continued, in spite of the "little taste of power" she had had, seemed rather appalling. "'It was also a great challenge. . . . Of course I accepted the challenge."[21]

In New York later that month she attended the meeting of League representatives to complete the structure of the new Federation. On January 20, 1899, at the Social Reform Club, the delegates elected Mrs. Lowell as president, Mary K. Simkhovitch first vice-president, Mrs. Henrotin second vice-president, John Seely-Ward treasurer, and Florence Kelley corresponding secretary. It was also decided "to employ Mrs. Kelley as an inspector and organizer, as soon as an annual payment of $3000.00 salary and expenses could be guaranteed by the National Federation for two years."[22]

Thus uncertain as to when her new duties would begin, Florence Kelley lost no time in exploring an alternative that lay equally close to her heart—an appointment as Factory Inspector of New York State. In his inaugural message on January 2, 1899, Theodore Roosevelt, newly-elected governor of New York, had hit hard at the sweatshops, and had proposed enlarging and revamping the Board of Factory Inspection.[23] Certainly, here

---

[21] Speech delivered at a banquet to honor John Graham Brooks, Hotel Vendome, Boston, Nov. 19, 1925. Box 6, Folder 16, NCL files.

[22] *Minutes*, Massachusetts Consumers' League, *op. cit.*, Jan. 26, 1899. Although the NFCL constitution names a General Secretary among the federation officers to be elected, Florence Kelley continued to be listed as Corresponding Secretary for several years. She appears for the first time as General Secretary in the *Sixth Annual Report*, Year Ending March 1, 1905.

[23] *State of New York, Messages of the Governors*, Vol. X, 1899-1906, ed. Charles A. Lincoln, Albany, 1909, pp. 7-9.

was an exceptional opportunity for a person of her qualifications and experience. On January 21 she dispatched a note to Roosevelt setting forth her request. On the same day, at her suggestion, Jacob Riis[24] also wrote to the Governor, backing up her application, as did Lillian Wald on the following day. Then, without waiting for a reply, Florence Kelley and Jane Addams, escorted by Riis, called on Roosevelt at his New York residence to discuss the matter directly.

The Governor was at home when they arrived, but was hurrying to keep another engagement, did not realize who the "two ladies" announced with Riis were, and refused to see them. When he discovered whom he had turned away, he hastened to send letters of apology to both Florence Kelley and Riis. By a curious mischance the letter to Florence Kelley apparently never reached her (for want of her own address, Roosevelt had sent the letter to Henry Street, in care of Lillian Wald). In it he expressed the fear that "your non-residence may be a bar to your appointment," but added, "I should greatly like to see you here . . . If you will write in advance . . . I will be at your convenience."[25]

To Riis he detailed at some length the difficulties such an appointment would entail:

> There will be two great practical difficulties about appointing Mrs. Kelley. The first is, she is not a New Yorker, and the second is, that to all the people who do not know (and they include practically everyone) the fact that she was appointed by Altgeld is a most tremendous handicap. Every enemy of the system would seize upon it at once and it would be impossible ever to get the matter entirely straight in their minds. Any recommendation she makes against the interests of the employers would be at once met by the cry that "this is Altgeldism." I do not mention this as influencing me at all, because her connection with Miss Addams and what you say, taken together, are quite

---

[24] Riis had been a police reporter when Roosevelt was Police Commissioner of New York, and had worked closely with him for some years. As a result, a warm, lasting friendship had developed. See Jacob A. Riis, *Theodore Roosevelt The Citizen*, New York, 1904.

[25] TR to FK, Jan. 23, 1899. No. 476, Theodore Roosevelt Letterbooks, Executive Official, Vol. I, Jan. 3-29, 1899, Library of Congress.

enough for me, but it would be a very serious detriment in any effort to accomplish good results.[26]

How much of Roosevelt's stand was based on political caution, how much of it was a reflection of his old dislike of Altgeld, is problematical. His letter to Riis closed by saying he would "see either or both of them [Mrs. Kelley and Jane Addams] any time they come up," but no further promise was made.

Not yet apprised of the contents of the letter to Riis, and buoyed up by the prospect of new horizons opening out, Florence Kelley returned once more to Chicago. To Lloyd she wrote on January 31:

> I have asked Governor Roosevelt to appoint me Chief Factory Inspector of New York. I am becoming a professional office-seeker. But it is only one kind of office I want; and I want it because, like my modest friend Mr. Bisno,[27] I am persuaded that no one else now in the field would work so effectively against the sweating-system as I could with Teddy to back me in my enforcement of the law. Bisno always wants to do things because no one else in sight will do them so well! There seems, however, to be a fighting chance for my getting the position. It runs three years; and I believe I could so disperse the sweaters from the surface of Manhattan that they could never reassemble, just as they can never again get a foothold in Massachusetts.

But the lack of response from Roosevelt worried her. For the next several weeks, while friends were making other efforts in her behalf, she wavered between lingering hope and the intuition that hers was a lost cause. To one of her friends she wrote on February 4:

> Lady Jane is to see Teddy at his house on the 17th in New York. I have abandoned all hope because Teddy has not answered my letter or taken any notice of my existence. He has, however, written Jacob Riis that while *he* Teddy has no prejudices, the community would object to an Altgeld appointee. Which, of course, may be true and is certainly polite and a tenable position. However, we know the persuasive qualities of the Lady . . . I am so possessed

---

[26] TR to Riis, Jan. 23, 1899. No. 401, *ibid.*

[27] Abram Bisno, who worked as a cloak-maker in Chicago, had been a deputy factory inspector under Florence Kelley.

by the magnitude of the opportunity that I can think of nothing else.[28]

Roosevelt produced a different set of reasons when Maud Nathan, as president of the New York Consumers' League, made a trip to Albany "confident that he would see the wisdom of appointing one so well equipped for the job." But while recognizing Florence Kelley's ability, and expressing sympathy generally with the aims of the League, the Governor

> was quite frank in pointing out . . . that the time was not ripe . . . to appoint a woman as factory inspector; . . . his constituents would not stand for it; they were urging him to appoint a certain man and nothing would be gained by opposing their wishes in the matter.

The Governor's frankness did not include the fact, according to Mrs. Nathan, that as far as qualifications went, his chosen appointee ran an elevator in Albany, and had secured preference through the influence of the legislature.[29]

A meeting between Jane Addams, again accompanied by Riis, and Roosevelt did take place at five o'clock on Friday, February 17, in New York. There is no record of the conversation, but, against the exigencies of politics, Miss Addams' persuasive qualities for once were unavailing.

Florence Kelley took the rejection of her application with good enough grace; there would still be plenty of work for her to do. Roosevelt was very much aware of the value of her attainments, and was careful to leave the way open for future and frequent communication—a situation of which she was to take full advantage during his term of office.[30]

While waiting out the results of her friends' efforts she had not been idle. Early in February, for example, she had made a trip to Cincinnati "to lecture and preach." But once she realized

---

[28] The letter is addressed only to "Dearly beloved," and is otherwise unidentifiable. Lady Jane is of course Jane Addams.

[29] Nathan, op. cit., p. 55. There is an ironic footnote to this episode. Shortly after Florence Kelley's return to New York to take up her League duties, Roosevelt wrote to the new factory inspector, John Williams, directing him to reach and talk to Mrs. Kelley because "She knows more about enforcing the factory law than any man I know of, and I want you to keep in touch with her." TR to John Williams, June 2, 1899. No. 404, TR Letterbooks, Vol. III, Mar. 24-July 5, 1899.

[30] "Dear Jake:—I thank you particularly for Mrs. Kelley's letter. It gives me exactly the working plan I wanted." TR to Riis, Jan. 17, 1900. TR Letterbooks, Jan. 8-Mar. 28, 1900. Her letter, dated Jan. 15, is not found.

that the factory inspectorship was not forthcoming, she was understandably anxious to hasten arrangements with the National Federation. In March she wrote a letter to the Massachusetts Consumers' League which, according to the Minutes (March 20) "strengthened the sentiment that her work should begin May 1." Miss Coman wrote back suggesting that Florence Kelley submit a plan of action on the Consumers' Label in time for a special Executive Committee to be held the middle of April in New York.

By April 7 she had sent a detailed draft to Mrs. Simkhovitch, "for the purpose of being blue-pencilled by the meeting and returned with additions, subtractions and modifications to be used by me as instructions." The draft was a four-point program which included scouting for factories worthy of the Consumers' Label, designing the label and registering it as a trade mark, making up an awards contract as between manufacturers and the League, and working out "a well-considered plan for advertising the label," especially among the buying public. It is "the woman enquiring for goods carrying the label," Florence Kelley emphasized, who after all will be the most effective advertiser.

The meeting, which she did not attend, was held on April 15 at 248 East 34th Street. Her program was accepted and she was appointed chairman of a committee of three (with power to name the other two) "to arrange all matters connected with the label." After the member Leagues had reported a series of financial guarantees, "It was voted that the President be empowered to pay our present secretary Mrs. Kelley" an annual salary of $1500 and necessary expenses, as "Inspector for the National Federation of Consumers' Leagues," to begin her duties on May 1.[31]

Her course at last determined, she had only to wind up her affairs in Chicago. Her library job would terminate on April 30.

---

[31] *National Consumers' League Minutes,* Council 1898-1904 (Executive Committee, 1899-1906), April 15, 1899. NCL files. At this meeting Dr. John Graham Brooks was elected president, replacing Mrs. Lowell, and Mrs. Nathan first vice president, replacing Mrs. Simkhovitch. The Federation was declared to consist of four state Leagues: New York, Massachusetts, Illinois and Pennsylvania. (Some months earlier it had been decided that Leagues formed in various towns and cities of a given state be considered branches of the state League; thus Syracuse and Brooklyn were now branches of the New York State League. Nathan, *op. cit.,* p. 68.) The name National Consumers' League was assumed some time between April 15 and May 1.

The children were still in school, but they would spend the summer with the Lloyds and join her in New York in the fall. All that remained was to clear out her room, close "the window overlooking the little court with the fountain," and be on her way, her face turned, as ever, toward the future.

The change in fortune could not have come at a more opportune time. Florence Kelley was now a woman of forty, mature in experience as well as intellect. At Hull House she had seen theory brought to life in the lives of the teeming thousands around her. In her new position she would have virtually unlimited freedom to make use of this tested synthesis of theory and action.

And make use of it she did. The broad and roving mandate given her by the League was admirably suited to a person of her temperament. The program under which she went to work was, in general, to build Consumers' Leagues and, in particular, to award the label to those cotton underwear factories that passed inspection. But her own underlying concept was far wider and more complex, and had its roots in her most cherished doctrine. "The work of the Consumers' League is an educational movement," she wrote in her Second Annual Report (1900) "as all-embracing as the need of civilized people for food, clothing and shelter." The many campaigns she engaged in, the various organizations and movements she helped found, or joined, or lectured to, or merely approved and encouraged, were all part of this educational network. Translated into economic, legislative and ethical pressures they must, she felt, bring about a happier social order.

At times the complaint was heard that she used her prerogative with more vigor than wisdom. Of course Florence Kelley made her share of mistakes, but she was never so wrong as she was right, and in the end even her enemies had to admit it. And while she may have antagonized some with her brusqueness, she more than made up for it by the singular purity of her adherence to principle.

There are a thousand stories, old and new, that friends remember. There was the time, on one of her lecture circuits, when the audience consisted of just one man. She went ahead with

Florence Kelley, about 1899

her talk as if he were a roomful; and when she returned from her tour, on her desk lay a check for $10,000 signed by her sole listener.[32] There was the time she attended a convention of the National Association for the Advancement of Colored People in Memphis. She had been assured that the convention would not be segregated, but then discovered that the Negro members were holding separate sessions in a Baptist church. As each speaker at the church rose in turn, he saw before him "a sea of dark faces and among them one white face—that of Florence Kelley."[33]

She adored her children. It cost her much to have to be separated from them, and her love and longing are woven into her letters: "I would give a good deal for a glimpse of the bloom of Ko"; "John is the light of my eyes. . . . He is not much of a scholar, but he is an adorable lad"; "Please give . . . my congratulations [to Mrs. Kautsky] upon the advent of her little daughter. If she proves as great a delight as my little Margaret, there is no other such happiness."[34] Late in 1904 she had gone up to Boston to visit Margaret, and the boys had come in from college to meet here there. "All Christmas day she sat with her children all over her," wrote Elizabeth Glendower Evans. "She said to me afterwards, 'You can't think what this Christmas means to me, to have my children, all of them with me. Such a thing has but rarely happened in my life.'"[35] Margaret's sudden death from a heart attack the following year was a blow from which Florence Kelley never fully recovered; yet for this grief too she was able to find a place, and to take up her work again.

More and more, as the years went by, her friends and co-workers came to rely on her as a never-failing source of energy and stimulation. "I have seen a dead Board galvanized," said Dr. W. E. B. Dubois at a celebration of her twenty-fifth year with the National Consumers' League, "sometimes quite un-

---

[32] Mrs. Karl Tausig (Louise G.), post-card, and telephone conversation, Apr. 21, 1961, and April, 1964. Mrs. Kelley told the story, in 1930 or 1931, to a gathering that had turned out to be disappointingly small.

[33] Interview with Mrs. Emily Sims Marconnier, Jan. 21, 1959.

[34] To Lloyd, Aug. 9, 1897; to Jane Addams, Aug. 28, 1899; to Engels, Dec. 31, 1894.

[35] "Interesting People I Have Known," in *Springfield Sunday Union and Republican*, Springfield, Mass., Sept. 16, 1934.

willingly, by her new queries, new orientation of thought, until we convinced Mrs. Kelley that our conclusions were right, or just as often until she had convinced us that we were not ready for conclusions at all." And Newton D. Baker, recalling her during the war years, wrote of her magnetic presence: "Everybody was brave from the moment she came into the room." It was this power to transmit her own inner strength to those around her that was perhaps her most effective trait.

"If our age were the Middle Ages," wrote John Haynes Holmes the day after she died, "the late Mrs. Kelley would be canonized and remembered as Ste. Florence." Such praise would surely have amused her. She would have smiled indulgently, and gone off on another of her endless rounds.

She left no monument, although the sheaf of laws that place a guarding hand between the child and the machine might serve, were her name engraved thereon. Someone once remarked that we live in the memory of our friends, and when they are gone, the record of our deeds lives on as memory.

Consider the record of Florence Kelley.

NOTE:

Mrs. Kelley's correspondence with Engels, together with some of the relevant material in this book, appeared as an article entitled '"Dear Mr. Engels": Unpublished Letters of Florence Kelley (-Wischnewetzky) to Friedrich Engels, 1884-1894', in the Spring 1964 issue of *Labor History*.

BIBLIOGRAPHY

I—LETTERS, FAMILY PAPERS AND OTHER PAPERS

Unpublished letters of William D. Kelley to his wife Caroline B. Kelley, 1871. In the possession of Mr. John Bartram Kelley.

Letters from Florence Kelley Wischnewetzky to Mary Thorn Lewis, Jan. to June, 1885. In the possession of Mr. Nicholas Kelley.

Letters from Florence Kelley-Wischnewetzky to Friedrich Engels, Dec. 5, 1884 to Dec. 31, 1894. On microfilm. From Archiv, IML, Fond I, Opis 5 (Archive, Institute of Marxism-Leninism, Fund I, Schedule 5). Moscow.

Letters from Florence Kelley (-Wischnewetzky) to Richard T. Ely. Richard T. Ely Papers, State Historical Society of Wisconsin, Madison, Wisc.

Letters from Florence Kelley (-Wischnewetzky) to Henry Demarest Lloyd. Henry Demarest Lloyd Papers, State Historical Society of Wisconsin.

Letters from Friedrich Engels to Mrs. Florence Kelley-Wischnewetzky, Feb. 4, 1885, to Jan. 12, 1889. In Friedrich A. Sorge Collection, Manuscript Division, New York Public Library. Of twenty-three letters and post-cards, nineteen are published in part or in full in *Letters to Americans, 1848-1895*, ed. Alexander Trachtenberg, tr. Leonard E. Mins. International Publishers, New York, 1953.

Bonsal Family Papers, Manuscript Collection, Columbia University Libraries.

Address written by Caroline Bartram Kelley for the Bartram Reunion, June 8, 1893 (Ms). Historical Society of Pennsylvania, Philadelphia, Pa.

Henry C. Carey Papers, Historical Society of Pennsylvania.

Miscellaneous papers and records, Archives, Cornell University, Ithaca, N. Y.

Jane Addams Papers, Swarthmore Peace Collection, Swarthmore College, Swarthmore, Pa.

Theodore Roosevelt Letterbooks (1899, 1900), Manuscript Division, Library of Congress, Washington, D.C.

National Consumers League Files, Manuscript Division, Library of Congress.

II—FLORENCE KELLEY'S WRITINGS

Partial listing, covering material referred to in the text.

"On Some Changes in the Legal Status of the Child Since Blackstone," *The International Review*, August, 1882.

"Need Our Working Women Despair?", *The International Review*, November, 1882.

181

Preface to *The Object of the Working Class* by Dr. Johann Jakoby, New York, 1887.

"The Need of Theoretical Preparation for Philanthropic Work," in Backus [Mrs. Helen Hiscock], *The Need and Opportunity for College Trained Women in Philanthropic Work*, New York, 1887.

Our Toiling Children, Woman's Temperance Publishing Association, Chicago, 1889.

"Die Lohnsklaverie der amerikanischen Kinder," *Die Neue Zeit*, Vol. 7, 1889. (Edited translation of *Our Toiling Children*.)

"White Child Slavery" (Contribution to A Symposium), *Arena*, Vol. 1, 1889.

"Child Labor," *Frank Leslie's Illustrated Weekly*, Feb. 1890.

"A Footprint in New York," *Workmen's Advocate*, Mar. 15, 1890.

"A Decade of Retrogression" (Contribution to A Symposium), *Arena*, August, 1891.

"Factory Legislation in Illinois," paper read at 7th Annual Convention of Factory Inspectors, in *International Association of Factory Inspectors of North America*, (Proceedings), 1893.

"The Need of Uniformity in Labor Legislation," paper read at 8th Annual Convention of Factory Inspectors, (Proceedings), 1894.

"Child Labor in Illinois," paper read at 9th Annual Convention of Factory Inspectors (Proceedings), 1895.

"The Sweating System," in *Hull House Maps and Papers*, New York, 1895.

"Wage Earning Children," (with Alzina P. Stevens), in *Hull House Maps and Papers*.

"Die Fabrikgesetzgebung der Vereinigten Staaten," in *Archiv für soziale Gesetzgebung und Statistik*, Berlin, 1895.

"The Working Child," paper read at 23rd Annual Conference of Charities and Corrections, in *Conference of Charities and Correction*, Boston and London, 1896.

"The Sweating System," paper read at 10th Annual Convention of Factory Inspectors, (Proceedings), 1896.

"Working Boy," *American Journal of Sociology*, November, 1896.

"Child Labor," *The Charities Review*, Vol. 6, #3, 1897.

"Die weibliche Fabrikinspektion in den Vereinigten Staaten," in *Archiv*, 1897.

"Evolution of the Illinois Child Labor Law," paper read at the 11th Annual Convention of Factory Inspectors, (Proceedings), 1897.

"Illinois Child Labor Law," *American Journal of Sociology*, January, 1898.

"The Working Woman's Need of the Ballot," summarized in Stanton, Anthony, Gage, *A History of Woman Suffrage*, Rochester, 1881-1902.

"Das Sweating system in den Vereinigten Staaten," in *Archiv*, 1898.

"Die gesetzliche Regelung der Kinderarbeit im Staate Illinois," in *Archiv*, 1898.

"Drei Entscheidungen Oberster Gerichte über den gesetzlichen Arbeitstag in den Vereinigten Staaten," in *Archiv*, 1898.

"The U.S. Supreme Court and the Eight Hours Law," in *American Journal of Sociology*, July, 1898.

"Hull House," *New England Magazine*, July, 1898.

"Das Gesetz über freis Volksbibliotheken des Staats Illinois," in *Archiv*, 1899.

"Die Italiener Chicagos," in *Archiv*, 1899.

"Das Fabrikinspektorat von New York und seine Stellung zur Arbeiterschutzgesetzgebung," in *Archiv*, 1901.

Some Ethical Gains Through Legislation, New York, 1905.

Modern Industry, in Relation to the Family, Health, Education, Morality, New York, 1914.

"Notes of Sixty Years," autobiographical sketches in *The Survey:* "My Philadelphia," Oct. 1, 1926; "When Co-education Was Young," Feb. 1, 1927; "My Novitiate," Apr. 1, 1927; "I Go To Work," June 1, 1927.

III—FLORENCE KELLEY'S TRANSLATIONS

The Condition of the Working Class in England in 1844 by Friedrich Engels, New York, 1887; London, 1892.

The Object of the Working Class by Dr. Johann Jakoby (Speech, 1870). New York, 1887.

Free Trade by Karl Marx (Speech to the Brussels workers, Jan. 9, 1848). Boston, 1888.

IV—FLORENCE KELLEY'S REPORTS

First Annual Report, Factory Inspectors of Illinois, Dec. 15, 1893 (Illinois, 1894).

Factory Inspectors Special Report on Smallpox—First Special Report, July 1, 1894 (Illinois, 1894).

Second Annual Report, Factory Inspectors of Illinois, Dec. 15, 1894 (Illinois, 1895).

Third Annual Report, Factory Inspectors of Illinois, Dec. 15, 1895 (Illinois, 1896).

Fourth Annual Report, Factory Inspectors of Illinois, Dec. 15, 1896 (Illinois, 1897).

V—NEWSPAPERS AND PERIODICALS

American Economic Association Publications
American Journal of Sociology
Archiv für soziale Gesetzgebung und Statistik
Arena
The Charities Review
The Christian Union (The Outlook)
The Congressional Record
The Cornell Daily Sun

The Cornell Era
The Cornell Review
The Hartford Courant
The Hartford Evening Post
The Intercollegiate Socialist
The International Review
The Ithaca Democrat
The Ithaca Journal
The New York Daily Tribune
The New York Herald
The New-Yorker Staatszeitung
The New York Times
The New-Yorker Volkszeitung
Die Neue Zeit (Zürich)
North American Review
The Philadelphia Evening Bulletin
The Philadelphia Public Ledger
Putnam's Monthly Magazine
Der Sozialdemocrat (Zürich)
Der Sozialist (New York)
The Survey
The Workmen's Advocate
Frank Leslie's Illustrated Weekly
The Woman's Journal

VI—CONVENTION PROCEEDINGS

Proceedings, American Federation of Labor Founding Convention, 1886.

Report of the Proceedings of the National Convention of the Socialistic Labor Party, held at Buffalo, N. Y., Sept. 17, 19, 20, 21, 1887. New York, 1887.

National Convention of Labor Bureaus, Proceedings, 1888-1891. Seventh Convention, June 25, 26, 27, 1889. Hartford, Conn., 1889.

Report of the Bureau of Labor Statistics—Connecticut. Hartford, Conn., 1889.

Convention Proceedings, International Association of Factory Inspectors of North America, 1893-97 inclusive.

Proceedings, National Conference of Charities and Correction, Boston and London, 1896.

VII—BIOGRAPHICAL DICTIONARIES, COMPENDIA, ETC.

A Biographical Album of Prominent Pennsylvanians, 1st series, 1888. American Biographical Publishing Co., Charles R. Dacon, mgr.

Biographical Dictionary of the American Congress, 1774-1961, Washington, D.C., 1961.

Brockett, L. P. *Men of our Day*, Philadelphia, 1872.

Dictionary of American Biography, Vol. X, New York, 1943.

Encyclopedia Britannica, New York, 1960.

Encyclopedia of the Social Sciences, vols. VII-VIII, New York, 1932.

National Cyclopedia of American Biography, vol. XXIII, New York, 1933.

Who's Who in New York, 1904, 1926.

Cornell *Register*, 1876-82.

Gopsill's *Philadelphia City Directory*

Trow's *New York City Directory*

VIII—BIOGRAPHY

Goldmark, Josephine. *Impatient Crusader*, Urbana, 1953.

IX—BOOKS AND PAMPHLETS

Addams, Jane. *Twenty Years at Hull House*, New York, 1910.

Adler, Viktor. *Briefwechsel mit August Bebel und Karl Kautsky*, Vienna, 1954.

A Memorial of Sarah Pugh, A Tribute of Respect from her Cousins, Philadelphia, 1888.

Anthony, Katherine. *Susan B. Anthony, Her Personal History and Her Era*, New York, 1954.

Autobiography of Andrew D. White, 2 vols., New York, 1922.

Aveling, Edward, and Eleanor Marx-Aveling. *The Working Class Movement in America*, London, 1888.

Bebel, August. *Aus Meinem Leben*. Hrsg. von Karl Kautsky, 3 vols., Stuttgart, 1914.

Becker, Carl Lotus. *Cornell University*. Six lectures delivered on the Messenger Foundation. New York, 1943.

Bernstein, Eduard. *My Years of Exile*, translated by Bernard Miall, London, 1921.

Booth, Charles, ed. *Labour and Life of the People*, with "Maps of London Poverty," London, 1891.

Browin, Frances Williams. *A Century of Race Street Meeting House*. Published by Central Philadelphia Monthly Meeting of Friends, Philadelphia, 1956.

Browne, Waldo R. *Altgeld of Illinois. A Record of His Life and Work*, New York, 1924.

Bruegel, Ludwig. *Geschichte der oesterreichischen Sozialdemokratie*, 5 vols., Vienna, 1922-25.

Campbell, Helen Stuart. *Prisoners of Poverty*, Boston, 1887.

Commons, John R. *History of the Labor Movement in the United States*, 4 vols., New York, 1918.

Contributions to Mechanico-Therapeutics and Orthopedics, ed. L. Wischnewetzky, M.D., Vol. I. No. 1, New York, 1891.

Croly, Jane Cunningham. *History of the Woman's Club Movement in America*, Pennsylvania, 1898.

Cromwell, Otelia. *Lucretia Mott*, Cambridge, 1958.

David, Henry. *History of the Haymarket Affair*, New York, 1936 (2nd ed. 1958).

De Mille, Anna George. *Henry George, Citizen of the World*. Edited by Don C. Shoemaker, introduction by Agnes De Mille, Chapel Hill, 1950.

Destler, Chester McArthur. *Henry Demarest Lloyd and the Empire of Reform*, Philadelphia, 1963.

Deutsch, Leo (Lev Grigor'evich Deich). *Sixteen Years in Siberia*, translated by Helen Chisholm, London, 1903.

Diamond Jubilee Pamphlet of the New Century Club, Philadelphia, 1957.

Ely, Richard T. *Ground Under Our Feet, An Autobiography*, New York, 1938.

———. *Socialism, an examination of its nature, its strength and its weakness, with suggestions for social reform*, New York and Boston, 1894.

Engels, Friedrich. *Aus der Frühzeit des Marxismus, Briefwechsel mit Kautsky*. Herausgegeben und erlautet von Karl Kautsky. Prague, 1935.

———. *Briefe an Bernstein*, Berlin, 1925.

———. *Paul et Laura Lafargue, Correspondance*, 3 vols., Paris, 1959.

Ensign, Forest Chester. *Compulsory School Attendance and Child Labor*, New York, 1921.

Fairchild, Fred Rogers. *The Factory Legislation in the State of New York*, New York, 1905.

Fine, Sidney. *Laissez Faire and the General Welfare State:* A Study of Conflict in American Thought, 1865-1901, Ann Arbor, 1956.

Foner, Philip S. *History of the Labor Movement in the United States,* Vol. II, New York, 1955.

George, Henry, Jr. *The Life of Henry George*, New York, 1900.

Ginger, Ray. *The Bending Cross*, New Brunswick, 1944.

Harper, Ida Husted. *The Life and Work of Susan B. Anthony*, 3 vols., Indianapolis, 1894.

Hart, Smith. *The New Yorkers*, New York, 1938.

Hewett, Waterman Thomas. *Cornell University*, 4 vols., New York, 1905.

Hicks, John D. *The Populist Revolt*, University of Nebraska Press, 1961.

History of the State of New York, New York State Historical Association, 10 vols., 1933-37, ed. Alexander C. Flick. Vol. VIII. Wealth & Commonwealth.

House Executive Documents, 53rd Congress, 2nd Session, Vol. 31, 1894.

House Miscellaneous Documents, 52nd Congress, 1st Session, Vol. 1, Washington, D.C., 1892.

Hull House Maps and Papers, New York, 1895.

Hurwitz, Howard L. *Theodore Roosevelt and Labor in New York, 1880-1900*, Columbia University Press, 1943.

Kautsky, Karl. *Erinnerungen und Erörterungen*. Herausgegeben von Dr. Benedikt Kautsky, 's-Gravenhage, 1960.

Kelley, William Darrah. *Letters from Europe.* Six letters written to the *Philadelphia Times* During the Summer of 1879, with notes by the Author, Philadelphia, 1879.

———. *The Old South and the New*, Philadelphia, 1888.

———. *Speeches, Addresses and Letters on Financial and Industrial Questions*, Philadelphia, 1872.

Lange, Helene, and Gertrud Bäumer. *Handbuch der Frauenbewegung.* Die Geschichte der Frauenbewegung in den Kulturländern, Berlin, 1901.

Letters and Diary of Laura M. Towne, edited by Rupert Sargent Holland, Cambridge, 1912.

Lloyd, Caro. *Henry Demarest Lloyd*, 2 vols., New York and London, 1912.

Ludlow, Helen. *Memoir of Mary Anna Longstreth, with sketch of her work*, Philadelphia, n.d.

Mary Anna Longstreth Alumnae Association, Vol. 3, *Record of Teachers and Pupils*, Philadelphia, 1899.

Mayer, Gustav. *Friedrich Engels*, London, 1936.

Meijer, Dr. J. M. *Knowledge and Revolution: The Russian Colony in Zürich, 1870-1873.* Publications on Social History. Issued by the Internationaal Instituut voor Sociale Geschiedenis, Amsterdam, 1956.

Messages from the Governor, vol. VIII, 1885-91; vol. X, 1899-1906; New York.

Nathan, Maud. *The Story of an Epoch Making Movement*, New York, 1926.

Nicolay, G. and John Hay. *Abraham Lincoln, A History*, 10 vols., New York, 1890.

Peck, Mary Gray. *Carrie Chapman Catt*, New York, 1944.

Memoirs of Dr. Joseph Priestley to the year 1795 written by himself; with a continuation to the time of his decease, by his son Joseph Priestley, London, 1806.

Nevins, Allan. *Abram S. Hewitt, with some account of Peter Cooper*, New York and London, 1935.

Oberholzer, Ellis Paxon. *History of Philadelphia*, Philadelphia, 1910.

Quint, Howard. *The Forging of American Socialism*, U. of S. Carolina Press, 1953.

Rice, Allen Thorndike (ed.). *Reminiscences of Abraham Lincoln by Distinguished Men of his Time*, New York, 1888.

Riis, Jacob. *Theodore Roosevelt The Citizen*, New York.

Sandburg, Carl. *Abraham Lincoln, The War Years*, 4 vols., New York, 1939.

Scudder, Vida D. *Socialism and Character*, Boston and New York, 1912.

Sorge, Friedrich A. *Briefe und Auszüge aus Briefe an F. A. Sorge u. a.*, Stuttgart, 1906.

Spühler, Dr. Willy. *100 Jahre Universität Zürich*, Zürich, 1932.

Stanton, Elizabeth Cady, Susan B. Anthony, Mathilda Jocelyn Gage. *A History of Woman Suffrage*, 4 vols., Rochester, 1881-1902.

Suhl, Yuri. *Ernestine Rose and the Battle for Human Rights*, New York, 1959.

Talbot, Marion, and Lois K. M. Rosenberry. *History of the American Association of University Women, 1881-1931*, Boston and New York, 1931.

Ware, Norman J. *The Labor Movement in the United States, 1860-1895*, New York and London, 1929.

Woodbridge, Alice L. *Report on the Condition of Working Women in New York Retail Stores*, New York, 1892.

Woods, Robert, and Albert J. Kennedy. *Handbook of Settlements*, New York, 1911.

Working Woman's Society. *Report of the Tenement Committee*, New York, 1892.

Zander, Dr. Emil Wilhelm. "Methods of Medico-Mechanical Gymnastics," in Emil Anders Gabriel Kleen: *Massage and Medical Gymnastics*, London, 1918.

INDEX

189